SELLER TO STELLAR

Joe's Story

CARL BROMER

JORDAN WINAR

Dayton, Ohio & Austin, TX

Seller to Stellar: Joe's Story
The Ultimate 17-Day Sales Playbook

Copyright © 2023 by Carl Bromer and Jordan Winar
Published by Stellar Sales Training, Inc., Dayton, OH
www.stellarsales.com
info@stellarsales.com

ISBN 978-0-9745736-4-9
Library of Congress Control Number: 2023907763

Cover design by Daniel Eyenegho: eyeneghodaniel@yahoo.com
Internal page design by Paul-Baillie-Lane: pblpublishing.co.uk
Card design by Mark Bromer: info@stellarsales.com

All rights reserved. No part of this book may be reproduced or transmitted in any form or by any means, electronic or mechanical, including photocopying and recording, or by any information storage and retrieval system, without permission in writing from the publisher.

This is a work of fiction. Names, characters, business, events and incidents are the products of the author's imagination. Any resemblance to actual persons, living or dead, or actual events is purely coincidental

All Scripture quotations, unless otherwise indicated, are from the Holy Bible, English Standard Version.® Copyright © 2001, 2011 by Crossway, a publishing ministry of Good News Publishers. Used by permission of Crossway. All rights reserved.

Printed in the USA
2023—First Edition

This book is absolutely brilliant. I can see every salesperson, no matter what their age or stage, diving into a copy of this and working through the 17-day program. The storyline is so congruent with your brand and zone of genius. Your focus on training others how to sell, and not just on product knowledge, will resonate with every entrepreneur and business owner.

Dr. Tracey Jones, MBA, PhD
President, Tremendous Leadership, Boiling Springs, PA

About ten years ago, the company I co-founded (Physician Technology Partners) was dying on the vine. We needed training to jump start our sales efforts. A friend connected me with Stellar Sales Training. Within just a few months, our sales began to grow almost exponentially. The principles and techniques taught in this engaging story are real-world things you can *do* — I have personally experienced it and have seen the results.

Brian Zimmerman, MD
CMIO — Microsoft/Nuance

This book is captivating. After completing each chapter, I was anxious to read the next. I really enjoyed the method of storytelling between Brad and Joe. Anyone who wants to be a better version of himself or herself needs a proven game plan ... *From Seller to Stellar* delivers it! This book gives more than the path to becoming a great salesperson or manager — It provides a path to find true happiness, purpose, and fulfillment in life. It has caused me to stop, pause, and look at how I approach sales. I'm happy to say I currently implement many of these systems and techniques ... But they're *all* critical! Missing *a single step* could hold you back from reaching the top 4%. Since completing the book I've been reevaluating how I should implement those missing steps as I work toward being *and staying* in the top 4%.

Craig Bramer, First in Transport
Owner/CEO, Phoenix AZ

I can honestly say your sales principles and techniques are very real world and effective. I heartily recommend them to others who are looking for honest and reputable training…

Lee Murray, executive vice president
Chattanooga area Chamber of Commerce

I was introduced to the Stellar Sales Training process in the 1980s shortly after college. Reporting up to a Sales VP who had been an electrical engineer — who had piloted a Phantom F4 fighter jet — was a little intimidating at first. As a rookie just beginning my career, I quickly benefitted from the methods, systems, and tools that are now explained in *Seller to Stellar*. Within a few years, I was closing more than $1 million in revenue each year in an industry where $200 thousand was considered "excellent." Embracing the Stellar process helped to set me on a trajectory of meaningful career successes. I grew into higher levels of leadership and was privileged to occupy and experience the CEOs office years later. If you have the desire to succeed in your career, grow as a leader, and tap into your real purpose in life, I urge you to read *(and execute)* the principles and techniques in Carl's and Jordan's book.

Jay Schindler, G2 Potential LLC,
Founder & Certified Professional Coach

Seller to Stellar is a compelling page-turner. The process detailed by Brad and embraced by Joe will help anyone live a better life regardless of their profession. Even though I've known and respected Carl Bromer for more than 40 years, and I'm familiar with the process he and Jordan teach, I highlighted something on almost every page. If you'd like to have an even more successful career, life, or even retirement, read this book. You'll be glad you did.

Rex Houze, Founder: Improving Performance & Results
Author: Getting Results Through Others
Allen, TX https://improve-results.com

In a culture where we establish identity and worth based on our vocation, this book, "Seller to Stellar — Joe's Story" is a great reminder of the truth. The message, based upon a Christian World View, reminds us that true wisdom in how you identify yourself and set goals is based upon God. This book brings these concepts into focus with real and practical lessons. "I was living to work instead of working to live" is the phrase that stood out to me. This book has helped me examine my work and personal life.

David Slyby, Sports Marketing Executive
Cedarville University Adjunct Professor
Personal friend of Carl Bromer

I just finished reading your new book, *Seller to Stellar* ... I love it! This book reads so easy ... I truly believe it will impact many people in ways that you may never know (this side of eternity). The thought of that makes me happy. I was reminded of things I learned many years ago. Things I have now re-polished and re-implemented. I can't thank you enough for that. May God bless this book so it can bless all who read it.

Jeff Rex, Bona USA, Jansan Sport Floors
East Division manager

Your new book is a great reminder of so many lessons I have learned from you over the years, as well as a gentle kick in the bottom of those where I have become lax. I read *Seller to Stellar* to get a good "feel" for this new method you are presenting. And I have to say — I LOVE IT!!! — Thank you. I'm truly grateful for the touch your techniques and processes have had and continue to have on my life. It is an honor to be your friend and your brother in Christ.

Michael Propst, Sales Director; Vernon Graphics & Promotions
30+ Years using *From Seller to Stellar* principles and techniques

"Seller to Stellar, Joe's Story" is a delightful, easy read story, packed with common sense, actionable, top 4% techniques. Knowing and working with Carl Bromer for over twenty-five years, we have trained and applied his "Natural Selling Process" with unparalleled and unmatched results. "Seller to Stellar" is a must-read for anyone considering a sales career or simply wanting to refresh their own "One Best Way" of Selling or "Life" Skills... Read this book; and learn from one of the best.

Peter V Gorka, National Sales Manager
The OPEX Corporation, Moorestown, NJ

Having suffered through innumerable sales training programs over my many years in sales, I can say without equivocation that your techniques and principles are the absolute best I have *ever* encountered. It is brilliant in its common-sense approach to the sales process.

Walter F Kylie, Director of Sales Cobb Galleria Centre, Atlanta

The story about the three brothers in Seller to Stellar has changed my life. I often ask myself, when working on a project, *"Is this where the third brother would have stopped?"* "What would he have done?" Both inspire me to do more, or confirm that I have done all I can do for now. I know you will enjoy meeting the third brother in Carl's and Jordan's book, Seller to Stellar. I practiced law as in-house counsel for twenty years and had my own private practice for ten. I use the principles in this book daily in performing my work as an attorney. The concepts are easy to understand and incorporate into your personal and professional life. I worked with Carl before my journey to law school almost forty years ago, and saw Carl apply the principles of this book to revolutionize our sales force.

Steven Compton, JD
Brentwood, TN

Contents

Foreword by Lynn Trainor 1

Introduction 3

Day 0: In the Beginning 5
Day 1: Starting the Journey 13
Day 2: Making Excellent Decisions Automatically 23
Day 3: Knowing Your Personal and Professional Lifetime Goals ... 29
Day 4: Replacing Time Management 41
Sunday Progress Review 49
Day 5: Building Thought–Habit–Action Patterns 55
Day 6: Developing the Most Critical Skill 65
Day 7: Creating Your Personalized Third-Brother Playbook ... 73
Day 8: Making the First Call on a New Contact 85
Day 9: Identifying Needs 97
Day 10: Qualifying—Finding the Real Needs 109
Day 11: Presenting 119
Day 12: Handling Objections 125
Day 13: Closing—Precipitating Action 135

Day 14: Measuring Quality   145

Day 15: Applying the Universal Law of Sales Success   159

Day 16: Completing the Challenge—What Now?   173

Day 17: Reaching True Top Four Percent Success   183

Epilogue   197

About the Authors   199

Acknowledgments   201

Testimonials   203

Foreword

Before retiring from the business world, I started and managed two successful high-tech companies. During my career, I experienced the gamut of motivational and sales training programs and books.

We all know the excitement that immediately results from a slick, fast-paced training seminar or a well-written book. However, we also know how quickly those "shots of excitement" fade when we return to our jobs and the reality of our daily routine retakes control of our everyday business lives. This book is not for you if you are wanting yet another magical shortcut or some "quick-read-to-success" book. Clearly, it is a quick read! But, to achieve results in your personal or business life, you will need to work with commitment and consistency to apply it.

Carl and Jordan's book is a refreshing treatment of a subject with timeless information. What's unique is the presentation format. Unfolding in an easy-to-read, conversational format, this book engages the reader in a seventeen-day adventure from the lives of two individuals—Brad the mentor, and Joe the salesman. Brad walks Joe through forty action steps that he promises will get Joe into the top four percent category of professional salespeople. Over these seventeen days, Brad reveals his techniques of working "smarter *and* harder," through goal setting, planning, organizing, executing, and activity management.

But don't expect to read this book and suddenly have instant success in your personal life or career! Brad freely gives you the techniques, but like Joe, you need to then invest your own time and commitment to internalizing these techniques into habits that will naturally guide your everyday life. In reality, most readers will likely never follow through with internalizing all of Brad's success techniques and advice—that's why 96 percent of salespeople never reach the top four percent. Only by working "smarter *and* harder" will you ever attain the top four percent status. It's your choice. If you are still reading at this point, there's a good chance you have what it takes to get into the elite top four percent.

I believe everything presented here is available to you through reading twenty to thirty books on related subjects. What's new here is the organization and crystallization of all these timeless success techniques, thus reducing them to forty action steps. Carl and Jordan have done this work of consolidation for you! And here, they have presented it in an engaging format that will hopefully help you attain your maximum potential in life.

I've known Carl Bromer for decades, and I have personally worked with him in one-on-one coaching sessions where he taught me virtually all the techniques revealed in this book. I have not met Jordan Winar, but based on Carl's comments, he also has achieved outstanding success using the principles and techniques in this book. I can guarantee you: This material has the potential to work for you too, but only if you are willing to invest your time and commitment to internalize it for your personal and business use.

One line in the book says: "There are only two ways to fail. One is to not start. And the other is to quit."

You have already started by reading this foreword. Now… don't quit!

Lynn Trainor

Retired CEO

Introduction

Do you ever feel you are doing everything you can to achieve success, but things just aren't working out the way you want? Do you want to be successful in your family and career, but for every two steps forward, it feels like you take three steps back?

Consider this fact: The most significant shared attribute of successful people in *every* family and *every* career field is their ability to make wise decisions consistently… and to influence other people to do the same. This crucial ability is the foundation of all success. Making wise decisions leads to success, and influencing others to do the same is what persuasion and selling are all about. It is also what this book is about!

Meet Joe

On the outside, he seems to have it all together, but on the inside, he's filled with confusion and turmoil. He doesn't have a clue what his next step in life should be. He likes the sales profession but wants to be better at it. In fact, he's felt this way most of his career. His results are mediocre at best. He feels like quitting.

Meet Brad

Over the last forty years, Brad and his company have developed, polished, and proven a remarkably effective and common-sense blueprint for a Sales Playbook. His people have achieved outstanding success using this blueprint to each develop their own custom Playbook. However, he's never shared their Playbook outside his company.

If a mentor, coach, or guide with decades of successful sales experience knocked on your door, would you listen to what they had to say? Joe is about to meet Brad for the first time. Joe's life will never be the same.

Follow Joe's lead, and your life will never be the same.

Day 0: In the Beginning

Joe couldn't sleep. He was worried about losing his job. If he didn't get his sales numbers up this quarter, he might get fired. Finally, after a number of restless hours, he got out of bed, dressed, and drove to his favorite twenty-four-hour diner not far from his home. Sitting there with his coffee, staring out the window at the dark, rainy, and quiet streets, he felt depressed and alone.

Yesterday—Monday—Joe, lost a huge sale—one that would have made his month, his quarter, *even* his year. He shook his head slowly and silently wondered, "What did I do wrong?"

Taking a sip of coffee, he sighed. His sales numbers had bottomed out over the last few quarters. He was tempted to blame all his problems and frustration on his company and his product… but deep down, he knew *he* was the one who needed to change; he just didn't know how. Feeling like a loser, he ran his hands through his hair. He worried about his bills, his marriage, what people thought about him… his future! And as if that wasn't enough, he needed to meet with his boss in a couple of hours to confess the gut-wrenching news of his lost sale.

Temporarily interrupting his pity-party, the server refilled his cup and asked if everything was OK. Joe looked up, gave a little smile as he nodded. The server returned the smile, turned, and walked away.

Feeling depressed, Joe stared into his steaming mug and muttered a prayer for help; not that he thought God cared about him. He shook his head, leaned back in the red vinyl booth, and sighed again. He hadn't even *thought* about God for a very long time.

Suddenly, someone tapped him on the shoulder. Startled, he turned to see an older gentleman who had been sitting at the end of the counter; now standing next to his booth, holding a cup of coffee.

"Sorry. Didn't mean to startle you. We've never met, but based on that sad look on your face, and the prayer I just heard, I'm guessing you've got some problems.

"My name's Brad Roberts. Mind if I sit down?"

Joe hesitated, but the stranger, dressed in a suit and tie, looked safe and sounded sincere, so he gestured for him to have a seat as he introduced himself. "Joe Daniel." He squeezed out a chuckle. "So, Brad Roberts, are you the angel God sent to help me?"

Brad looked Joe in the eye. "No, I'm no angel. Just an old man who saw a young man looking tired and depressed and possibly feeling sorry for himself." Brad looked down as he wrapped his hands around his warm coffee mug. Then, looking back up, "Tell me, Joe, what's weighing so heavy on your mind?"

Joe assumed he'd probably never see Brad again, so he took a chance and unloaded his problems on the mysterious and disarming stranger. "I'm so frustrated! I've been selling for years, but my sales have never been better than average. Now… I'm worried about losing my job… I could lose everything."

Joe stopped talking and broke eye contact, looking down momentarily. "Hey, I'm sorry, Mr. Roberts. I don't even know you, and here I am dumping my problems on a complete stranger."

Brad smiled warmly. "Please, call me Brad."

Joe felt some of his anxiety fade as he shared his problems with Brad. He hadn't even told his wife how bad things were.

Brad hesitated a moment, then said, "Joe, I've been in business for over fifty years, and I've seen a lot of problems." He spread his arms wide and then dropped them to the table. "We all have problems! Problems with family, kids, customers, employees, supervisors, government regulations, product quality, production, competition… you name it."

Brad leaned back in the booth. "You mentioned the problem involved your ability to sell. So, what's causing the problem?"

"That's what's so frustrating… I don't know! I'm not hitting my sales targets, and I just lost a huge sale. I think our products and services are good; our systems and our people are stellar… Sure, we have a few internal issues, but no more than any other company."

Brad raised a thumb. "So, if it's not the product—" Then he raised the next three fingers, one at a time. "—and it's not the service, systems, or people… what *is* causing the problem?"

Joe looked down in embarrassment. "I'm ashamed to admit it, but I'm starting to think *I'm* the problem!"

Brad tapped the table and smiled. "Recognizing the problem is the first step to solving it. It's an old cliché, but it's true. So, if *you* are the problem, let me ask one more time, *what's causing it?*"

Joe thought for a moment and then sheepishly admitted, "You know, Brad, I think I've lost confidence in my ability to sell. When I started this job several years ago, I went through some company-sponsored training. It focused on products and services, but not on selling. The higher-ups in our company seemed to think our products and services would sell themselves. All we needed were knowledgeable salespeople serving as ambassadors, literature dispensers, and living advertisements."

Joe's experience was affirmed by Brad's nod. "I understand. My company made the same mistake. We assumed the salespeople we hired needed product training more than sales training. We also assumed they had good sales skills, because they were likeable and well-dressed, and they could carry on a coherent conversation. But we were wrong. Even though we trained our salespeople, they were *not* trained!"

Joe's brow furrowed in confusion. "What do you mean?"

Brad explained, "Let me tell you a story. When I was about ten years old, my parents gave me a dog—a Border Terrier named Gus. Boy was he smart! I worked for years training my little buddy to speak English."

Joe laughed, but he immediately sensed Brad might be serious. "Sorry. I'm listening."

"You see, Joe, even though I trained him for years, Gus never spoke a word of English. I *trained* him, but he was *not trained!*

"Similarly, most people think exposure to training material and years of experience will lead to trained salespeople. I exposed my dog to the spoken word and a million instructions. He *understood* a lot of words. He could sit, shake hands, roll over, and fetch, but he never spoke. Even though I *trained* him to speak English—he was *never* actually *trained*… to speak English!"

At this point, Joe wasn't sure if Brad was being profound or insulting, so he nodded to show he was listening, but kept his thoughts to himself.

Brad went on. "Of course, a dog doesn't have the *ability* to speak, no matter how much training he has. You said you've been selling for years, so you must have the ability to sell; so, something must be missing in your training."

"I get what you're saying… I think." Joe rubbed his cheek and realized he hadn't even shaved that morning.

"Let me put it this way, Joe. We sent our people to sales training classes, but the training was a waste. We stuffed as much product knowledge into them as we could, but we never taught them *how* to sell.

"That's why, about forty years ago, we started developing our own training program—not just to *train* salespeople in the basics, but to make sure they were trained to succeed in selling. We worked on the program for almost thirty years… refining, testing, and polishing it repeatedly. Then, about ten years ago, our sales started growing exponentially. We felt like we had cracked a secret code… but actually, we found it wasn't a secret at all—it was basic logic! And remarkably simple! Now, we have each new hire work the program and these last ten years have been incredible."

Joe looked down for a moment, then back to Brad, and shook his head in amazement. "It took you forty years to come up with a sales plan? I think I might need something a little quicker."

Brad leaned forward… "Actually, it only took thirty years." Both men laughed. "The last ten years, we've been refining and polishing… but mostly, we've been enjoying the results. We have the proof. It works! Now, we have a *real* training program that works, and it only takes seventeen days!"

Joe felt energized by Brad's sincerity. Maybe he could improve; maybe it wasn't too late to save his job and his career. "So, what you're saying is, I'm not trained, so *I'm* the problem, and *you* are the solution?"

"Yes, you're the problem, Joe, but no, I'm not the solution."

"So, if you're not the solution, what is?"

Relaxing his shoulders, Brad leaned forward with a serious look on his face. "Think about it. If you're the problem, and I'm not the solution, who *is* the solution?"

Suddenly, as Joe stared into Brad's eyes, he realized what Brad was saying.

"So Brad, you're saying *I'm the solution?*"

"You know the answer, don't you?" Brad smiled. "I could see the lightbulb go on over your head."

"You're serious? Your program only takes seventeen days?"

"That's right, seventeen days. But you don't have to do it alone. I'm willing to help if you'll let me."

By now, Joe was intrigued by this mysterious *seventeen-day program*, but also a little wary. "Is this something your company sells?"

Brad shook his head. "No, it's just something we do internally. We've never shared the program outside our company."

Joe wasn't sure if it was his curiosity, fear, or desperation, but he believed this guy. Brad appeared to be genuinely sincere. "Can you tell me more about it?" Joe sipped his coffee which was almost cold now. He waved for a refill.

Brad hesitated, and then said, "I think this program might be why God put me on this earth, Joe. But before I go into details, let me ask you a question: How serious are *you*?"

Without hesitation, Joe answered, "I'll gladly pay you to coach me through the process."

"The only financial cost to you, Joe, is if you don't let me help you."

Joe spread his hands. "Why me?"

"I see a hunger in your eyes, Joe. But know this, even though we don't sell the program, there is a cost. You'll have to put in some serious work! And if you're willing to commit to the full seventeen days... each day except Sundays, completing a few assigned tasks each day, I can pretty much guarantee you'll succeed in sales—and not just sales, but in all areas of your life."

Joe felt a combination of excitement, skepticism, and curiosity. Excitement because Brad seemed like an answer to his prayer, skepticism because he knew the road to success wasn't some magic trick—It would take a lot of hard work. Yet he was curious because Brad seemed so confident in his seventeen-day program.

Deciding to go for it, Joe said, "If you're willing to show me the process, I promise I'll give it my best effort."

Brad offered his hand to Joe. "Are you sure you're up for the challenge?"

Without hesitation, Joe shook Brad's hand, knowing in his gut it was the right thing to do. "Absolutely!"

"Excellent," Brad said. "Tomorrow morning, we'll begin at five-thirty. Get some rest tonight. You're going to work and think very hard for the next seventeen days."

Brad stood to leave. "Your first assignment is due tomorrow when we meet. Write a short one-page description of the person you want to become. As you do, be sure to address the following questions: How does this future successful Joe Daniel behave? How does he dress and act? What has he achieved? Why is he so successful? Then make a list of improvements you can make to become that person. We'll talk about it tomorrow morning."

Brad turned and paid for his coffee at the counter, then smiled and nodded at Joe as he pushed open the glass door and departed.

The sun was bright now, and the café was busy with people talking, laughing, and placing their orders. Joe hadn't even noticed the activity as he talked to Brad. His mind was racing. He was still worried about how his boss was going to react to the lost order, but now he was excited about the strange encounter with the older man—a man who noticed him drowning and threw out a lifeline.

He smiled, eager to work on his first assignment.

Day 1: Starting the Journey

5:30 a.m.

Joe awoke earlier and more excited than usual, anticipating his first morning with Brad.

Driving to the diner, he had feelings that reminded him of when he was a child on Christmas morning, running down the stairs to find gifts overflowing under a twinkling tree. He pulled into an open parking spot near the diner door. He felt much better than he had the day before. Better for two reasons. First, his boss had not been nearly as critical or upset about the lost order as he had feared. Second, he had what he believed was an excellent response to Brad's first assignment.

Joe entered the diner and saw Brad already enjoying his coffee and reading the morning newspaper. As he walked over to Brad, he was excited—a big change from the day before.

Brad, gesturing for Joe to have a seat, said, "You're looking pretty chipper this morning!"

As Joe scooted into the booth, Brad asked the server to bring another cup of coffee for his new friend. Then Brad smiled at Joe. "You look exactly the way I had hoped you would for our first day—eager, hopeful, excited, and determined. Am I right?"

Handing a file folder to Brad and smiling in return, Joe responded, "You bet! My completed assignment is in that folder and ready for your review. And I'm ready for the next step."

Brad set the folder aside and asked, "What did you learn?"

Joe was stunned! Brad seemed to ignore his folder… his work!

Like a deer in the headlights, Joe's eyes widened, and he didn't immediately answer. Then, after a brief pause, he slowly responded, "Brad, you asked me about the person I want to become, but now you're asking me: 'What did I learn?'" He furrowed his brow, shot Brad a puzzled look, and tapped his finger on the table. "I did the assignment. I wrote a detailed description of the person I want to become. I described how this new me behaves, what I've achieved, and why I'm so successful. Then I listed a bunch of improvements I need to make to become this new person. So, Brad, I guess I learned a bunch of things I'm not… and a number of new things I need to do to become the man I want to be."

Brad placed his hand on Joe's file folder and asked, "How did the results of your assignment make you feel?"

Joe thought for a moment, then responded, "When I started working on the assignment, I felt overwhelmed. At first, it seemed like a huge project that would take forever to complete. But the more I wrote, the more I found the answers were fairly short. When I finished, I was motivated and energized. And then, when I woke early this morning, I felt a new excitement about my job and my life."

Brad's face lit up as he smacked the table and exclaimed, "Yes!" A bit of coffee spilled from both mugs, and everything got quiet for a few seconds as people turned to see what was happening. "That's excellent, Joe. Yesterday, you were slouched over in this booth, looking defeated, but today you look like a new man. Your circumstances haven't changed, but your perspective *has!* Joe, you're ready for the first lesson, and we don't even need to look in the folder to accomplish it."

Brad slid the unopened folder back to Joe. "Hang on to this. We'll be using it later in the program." Then he pulled a card out of his suit pocket and handed it to Joe, who read it out loud.

Third-Brother Action Step #1

*Never do less than asked.
Always do more than expected.*

Joe's first reaction was frustration. He had hoped for something significant—maybe even earthshaking—a secret that would accelerate him toward sales stardom. But all he got was a card about doing more than expected!

Looking at Brad, Joe shrugged as he asked, "Third-brother action step?" Then he set the card on the table and settled back in the booth, waiting for Brad's answer.

"Let me explain." Brad responded, "Many years ago, there were three brothers who worked for the same company. Each was a college graduate and had started at about the same salary. But a few years later, one earned a modest wage, one earned a good income, and the third earned well into six figures a year.

"Soon after they started working, their company needed a new supplier for some critical raw materials. The general manager asked each of the three brothers to help identify *and* qualify a new source.

"The first brother called the general manager later the same day to report he had found three possible suppliers and would forward their names. In effect, he identified three possible sources, but he did *not* qualify them.

"The second brother called the general manager shortly after the first brother, saying he located three possible sources, but was waiting for their bank credit reports to know which might be best. He followed up the next morning and gave his recommendation. Like the first brother, he identified three possible sources, but he took a little extra time to qualify them.

"The third brother, who now earns more than the other two combined, asked if he could have until the end of the week to complete the task. When he reported to the general manager several days later, he said he had contacted *seven* potential suppliers and asked each to send samples of their products. He received samples from five of the seven and quickly eliminated the other two as nonresponsive. He then forwarded the samples to an independent testing laboratory. As a result, three more suppliers were disqualified for quality reasons. "He then contacted the two remaining suppliers and requested quotes. The third brother also found evidence of a possible shortage for the product in the near future, so he asked the supplier with the best proposal if he could place an order for a large quantity, contingent on gaining his company's approval within twenty-four hours. The supplier agreed, and the third brother immediately called the general manager with his report and asked for permission to place the order.

"The third brother gave *everything* the general manager needed to make a good decision. He identified and qualified a great new supplier; and he also helped his company avoid a potentially severe problem by getting a delivery commitment *before* the order was even signed.

"You see," Brad continued, "the first brother *did not do* what he was told. The second brother *did only* what he was told. But the third brother *did more* than he was told. He anticipated what else would be needed; he was creative, a self-starter, and working on his own initiative, completed the task thoroughly *without* being told."

Raising his eyebrows, Brad asked, "The three brothers were given the same task; why did they respond *so* differently?"

This sounded like a simple question, but Joe didn't have an answer.

After a brief but uncomfortable pause, Brad continued, "Good decisions aren't automatic or magic. Most people are like the first two brothers. They never trained their brains to react with a good decision-making process. As a result, their decisions were not the best. However, the third brother had trained his brain to make—*and implement*—wise choices."

Brad paused, giving Joe a minute to process the story. Then he pointed at Joe's folder and said, "Success is all about making excellent decisions... *and* doing more than you're told! Before we go any further, I need you to decide which of the three brothers you're going to be."

Joe looked him in the eye. "Is this a trick question?"

Brad smiled as he raised his eyebrows, but didn't respond.

"The third brother obviously made the best decisions and delivered the best results. Of course, I want to be the third brother."

"Excellent!" Brad gave a thumbs-up. "A commitment to be the third brother is important.

"Joe, have you ever heard of the Pareto Principle? It's the 'eighty-twenty' rule."

Joe nodded. "Sure, but how does it relate to the third brother?"

"The Pareto Principle isn't a hard-and-fast mathematical law," Brad said. "It's more of a rule of thumb that says eighty percent of results come from twenty percent of the effort or cause. When my company checked our sales numbers, we found that eighty percent of our results were, indeed, coming from only twenty percent of our sales force! These were our top performers."

Joe slowly shook his head and said, "I understand the eighty twenty rule, but again, what's this got to do with the third brother?"

Brad's smile got even bigger as he said, "That's when we had a breakthrough! We took our top performers—the top twenty percent of our sales force—and applied the same eighty-twenty rule to them. What we surfaced was a very elite group of individuals—the top twenty percent of our top performers—in other words, the top four percent of our total sales force! This top four percent was generating about eighty percent of the total sales made by our top performers. That means the top four percent were bringing in about sixty-four percent of our total sales.

"We took those 'top four percent producers' and studied their day-to-day behavior so we could develop a program to replicate their results. That was when we realized, not only were these our best—our top four percent—salespeople, they were also consistently demonstrating third-brother behavior. Essentially, Joe, we discovered that the top four percent of our salespeople were functioning just like third-brothers.

"We compiled everything we learned, and the result is what we call our *Third-Brother Playbook*. It's a step-by-step guide to our seventeen-day program. It'll help you focus your activities and quality so you can grow into that elite top four percent. Simply stated, Joe, the goal of our seventeen-day program is to guide you into the top four percent of salespeople."

Shaking his head, Joe responded, "Sounds too good to be true. How soon can I get a copy of this playbook?"

Brad answered, "Whoa! Pump the brakes a little. This is Day 1. We still have groundwork to lay. Days 2 through 6 are the critical foundation for the playbook, and for your success. Then you'll be prepared for your personal copy of the playbook on Day 7."

Skeptical, Joe pushed back on Brad's statement. "You really think your program can do that in only sixteen more days?"

Brad nodded. "I have the results to prove it, but before we go forward, let's get back to the big order you lost. Why did you lose it?"

Joe thought for a moment, then with a touch of sarcasm replied, "I assume you're going to say my competition made better decisions and did more than they were told."

Brad's face lit up. "You're right! But I prefer to say, your competition *out-served* you. That's what happened to the first two brothers." Brad pointed to the Action Step #1 card. "They were out-served by the third brother because he made better decisions and did more than he was asked to do."

"Wait a minute!" Joe interrupted, "You're saying the first two brothers made *bad* decisions? I can't imagine they did it on purpose. I doubt they woke up that morning and said, 'I'm going to work, and I plan to make bad decisions.'"

"Actually, Joe, that *is* kind of what I'm saying! But let me explain. The two less successful brothers didn't wake up one day and suddenly *decide* to make *bad* decisions. However, at the subconscious level, they never trained their brains to make *good* decisions. They developed poor subconscious decision-making templates early in their lives and never changed them. Today, in most companies, it's still true… four percent of salespeople generate about two-thirds of all sales. The remaining 96 percent only generate about one-third of sales. You see, Joe, the bottom 96 percent still make decisions the same way they did in high school and college.

"Each of the brothers developed his personal decision-making template early in life. We call these decision-making templates: *Thought-Habit-Action Patterns*. Each of the three brothers now has his Thought-Habit-Action Patterns—*his early-life decision-making templates*—controlling his response to assignments. The three brothers made decisions daily, and those decisions shaped their days and months… even their whole lives!"

Brad paused and took a sip from his mug. "Please understand, the sum of a person's decisions—both good and bad—determines his or her success. When people get fired, some rise and chase down success, others get upset, some quit or settle for less, and some even score a DUI… It's a choice.

"You decide who your friends are, how you spend your time, what you think, feel, do, say, and learn. You decide the skills to develop. Your decisions determine who you are and how successful you'll be. Now, here's the question: Are you ready and willing to make hard third-brother decisions? Or will you go for easy ones like the first two brothers?"

Joe hesitated before nodding. "Okay, so everyone knows that making good decisions is important. You're saying my decisions are controlled by my habits—habits that were programmed into my subconscious? Can you give me an example?"

Brad responded by saying, "Sure… Complete the following three sentences as quickly as you can. Three strikes and you're… "

"… out." Joe didn't hesitate.

Then Brad said, "Your price is too… "

"… high!" Joe quickly responded.

Next, Brad asked, "Why should I pay that much?"

Joe looked at Brad and opened his mouth, but nothing came out. His brain seemed to be stuck in a mental vapor lock.

After a few seconds, Brad asked, "Joe, you had automatic responses for the first two things I said, but none for the third. How come?"

Joe shrugged. "I don't know."

"Listen carefully. At some point in your life, you were subconsciously programmed to automatically complete the first two sentences, but apparently not the third. You've developed *Thought-Habit-Action Patterns* for the first two statements only."

Joe leaned his elbows on the table. "OK, I agree it's important to have answers to typical questions, but what I really need to know, Brad, is how do I get from where I am into that top four percent?"

Gesturing with open hands, Brad answered, "It's quite simple. All you have to do is program your brain with the process for making excellent decisions and then follow up consistently with action like the third brother."

Joe shook his head. "Sounds simple, but in real life, I don't think it's that easy."

"You're right Joe, it is simple, and it's not easy… but it's not as hard as failure! You're already one day closer to the top four percent, and I'm confident you'll succeed. We'll dig deeper into Thought-Action-Habit Patterns later."

Brad pointed to the Action Step #1 card as he reminded Joe, "Never do less than asked. Always do more than expected. Each day, from now on, I'll give you a new card—some days, more than one. Some assignments will take longer, but most will only take about an hour—give or take a few minutes. Then, during the balance of the day, I want you to put into practice the new things you're learning.

"As we go through the program, the goal is to look at *all* the skills necessary to get into the top four percent. Some skills you may already have; others you'll need to develop. Some new skills will be easy to develop; others will take a third-brother effort."

Brad picked up the check for their coffees. "Let's continue meeting here in the morning at five-thirty. We'll have the same basic agenda each day. First, I'll ask what you learned. Then we'll talk, and I'll give you the lesson for that day. Finally, at six-thirty or so, I'll challenge you with an assignment to be completed before our next meeting. It won't be easy, but Joe, it *will* be worth it!"

Brad then added, "Your assignment yesterday was to describe who you want to become. That's your vision statement. Without a clear vision, Joe, people never make it to the top twenty percent… much less the top four percent.

"Your assignment for tomorrow is to rewrite your vision statement in a way the third brother would have written it. You need to have a clear vision for one year and three years into the future. People tend to overestimate what they can do in a year and underestimate what they can do in three. So, think it through as you rewrite it."

Brad stood to leave and offered his hand to Joe. "Are you still in?"

Joe shook the older man's hand and replied, "One hundred percent!"

Day 2: Making Excellent Decisions Automatically

5:30 a.m.

Joe walked into the diner with his shoulders back, folder in hand, and immediately spotted Brad smiling back at him from the same booth as the day before. Two cups of steaming coffee had already been poured.

"Good morning, Brad!" He gestured toward the closest mug. "Is this for me?"

Brad nodded. "I took the liberty of ordering for you."

"Thank you."

Brad nodded to acknowledge Joe's appreciation before saying, "I see you have your vision statement. What did you learn from this assignment?"

Handing his folder to Brad, Joe beamed. "I'm glad you had me rewrite the vision statement. It seemed to come alive in my imagination. I started seeing myself accomplishing great things. I felt more motivated than I have in a long time. It was exciting. It solidified what you said yesterday about a vision.

"Now I know, Brad, if I'm going to create the life I want, I need to start with a clear vision. I need to *see* my goal. When I rewrote my vision, I started feeling good about my dreams again."

"Excellent! You're already doing more than expected—like the third brother. Today, I want to share another thing he did… he made consistently excellent decisions."

"For the balance of our program, Joe, we'll focus on creating the *habit* of making excellent decisions. One of the most significant characteristics of people in the top four percent is their habit of making great decisions automatically—without second-guessing themselves."

Joe grinned. He had a good feeling that Brad was the answer to the half-hearted prayer he muttered just two short days ago. He was excited, feeling he was about to receive the map to success that he needed.

"I knew you had what it takes to succeed," Brad continued. "Making excellent decisions isn't magical or mystical, Joe. In fact, you already do *some* of it every day! I'll prove it. But first, I have a question: How much better do you think you would have done in sales, and in your personal life if *all* your critical decisions for the past ten years had been consistently excellent?"

"Ten years of great decisions? I'd probably own the company by now," Joe smiled with confidence.

Brad laughed, "Well, I can't promise you'll ever own the company, but I believe you have the ability to develop your skill even more! When that happens, you'll be knocking on the door of the top four percent."

With a surprised look, Joe asked, "You're saying I already have the ability to develop decision-making habits that will move me into the top four percent of sales reps?"

"You do! But now, let's prove it. Do you have a cell phone?"

"I have two!" Joe shrugged.

"What do you do when you want to call a friend?"

Pausing momentarily, Joe answered, "If it's a good friend, I probably have the number programmed into my personal phone. I simply tell my phone who to call or hit the shortcut button and they answer. Or I might get voicemail."

"Is using a telephone *critical* in your life?"

"Is this another trick question?" Joe asked. "Yes, it's absolutely critical. I can't imagine my life without a cell phone!"

"And yet, you not only have numbers programmed into your telephone, but you also have the procedure for using your telephone programmed into your brain. You don't even think about calling someone; you just do it. You might say you're automatically making excellent decisions without thinking every time you use your cell phone."

Hesitating, Joe nodded and said, "Yeah, but that's a pretty basic thing."

Then Brad asked. "How basic was it when you first got your cell phone?"

"Well, it took a couple of days to get used to it," Joe said. "Where are you going with this? Working with a cell phone is easy; working with unpredictable people is more of an art. A cell phone process is predictable; people aren't!"

Brad continued. "Okay, let's think about this. Using a cell phone is one of the countless critical tasks you perform every day: driving a car, baking your favorite cake, going to a restaurant, lifting weights, playing an instrument, attending to a crying baby or an upset client. All of these have one thing in common. They all seemed difficult until you trained your brain and developed your physical skills. Then, at some point in time, they became second nature and easy. They became subconscious habits."

"Hang on," Joe interrupted, "I agree that driving a car, following a recipe, or playing an instrument were hard at first, and I agree, I did develop subconscious habits. But your last example—attending to an upset client—is *not* the same!"

Brad acknowledged Joe's frustration. "Joe, it *is* the same… and that's the skill we start training in a couple of days. You've gone your whole life without that skill. Are you willing to give it a few more days to learn it at the proper time?"

"I suppose, but why not now since we're on the topic?" Joe answered, a bit frustrated.

"Because there's a time and a place for everything. You crawl before you walk, and you walk before you run. There's a logical sequence.

We've developed and tested what we're convinced is the best sequence for learning the skills used by the top four percent.

"Before we go too far, though, you need to know it won't be easy at first. It'll take time and practice. You may get frustrated! And you might even want to give up. But if you're truly committed, you'll hang in there. So let me ask, Joe, are you willing to hang in there? Are you willing to train your brain to respond to every person automatically and excellently in every situation?"

This time, Joe nodded with enthusiasm. "If you can teach it, I can learn it."

Brad gave a little fist pump as he said, "Excellent decision! You're committed to developing the habit of always making the right decision. So, let's look at what makes a decision 'excellent' and how to get started. Your enthusiasm already has you on the right path. Our process will take you the rest of the way."

Brad reached into his shirt pocket, pulled out a card as he did the day before, and slid it across the table to Joe, who then read it out loud.

Third-Brother Action Step #2

Be the Third Brother

Identify and build good habits today
that will accelerate your progress
toward worthwhile goals.

"Simply stated, Joe, making automatic, excellent decisions is a good habit *if* it moves you closer to worthwhile goals. We'll cover goals more in-depth tomorrow. For now, let's agree on this point: If you make excellent decisions automatically, you'll make better progress toward your goals!"

"Brad, you're saying my best progress toward my goals will come from habits that automatically push me to say and do the right things, at the right time, in the right way?"

Brad gave two thumbs-up. "You got it! Now let's talk about tomorrow's assignment. You've already written a description of the person you want to be. In addition to *who* you want to become, your assignment is to add the personal and professional goals you'll need to accomplish to *become* that person.

"Keep in mind, your *personal* goals are more important than your professional goals.

Looking confused—Joe asked, "Aren't they equally important?"

Brad shook his head. "Actually, Joe, the only reason you even *have* professional goals is to support your pursuit of personal goals. Start thinking of your professional goals as stepping stones to your personal goals."

Joe nodded silently, realizing this mind-blowing yet simple truth—his whole reason for working was to accomplish personal goals.

Brad finished his coffee and glanced at his watch. "Joe, I need to leave soon. But before I go, I want to acknowledge something. I know we haven't looked inside your folder. You might even be a bit frustrated with your progress. But keep in mind, the tallest buildings need the deepest and most solid foundations. Implementing a program that will take you into the top four percent requires a solid foundation as well.

"You'll also need a plan to take you from the foundation to the top. We started building the foundation the morning we first met. Hang in there for the next few days, and you'll have the completed foundation, the plan, and everything you need to make it to the top."

Brad stood to leave. "You know, Joe, our meetings every morning are optional. You can quit any time. But keep in mind, there are only two ways to fail. One is to never start. The other is to quit! You blew the first opportunity to fail when you started. Now, the only way to fail is to give up."

He looked Joe straight in the eye. "But I know you're not going to quit. Remember, your assignment for tomorrow is to write your list of goals we just talked about. I'll see you tomorrow."

Day 3: Knowing Your Personal and Professional Lifetime Goals

5:30 a.m.

Joe arrived a little earlier to surprise Brad with coffee the way he liked it—two creams, one sugar. But as he approached the diner, he looked in the window and saw Brad already seated in their usual spot, reading a book with a mug of coffee in hand. The book appeared quite small and old. Joe opened the door, and the small bells jingled to announce his arrival.

Brad looked up and smiled. Then, setting the book aside, he turned toward the counter and motioned for the server to bring Joe's coffee.

After a quick exchange of greetings, Joe asked, "What were you reading?"

"Oh, it's a little King James Bible my wife gave me many years ago. I like to read a few passages before I start each day."

"So, you're pretty religious?" Joe asked.

Brad smiled and softly responded, "No, not really. Maybe someday I'll share a little more, but for now, let's talk about getting you into the top four percent. Your assignment was to add a list of your professional and personal goals to your folder."

"Done!" Joe said, sliding his folder over to Brad,

"What did you learn this time?" Brad took a sip of coffee.

Joe didn't hesitate. "I learned that my goals are generic—pretty much the same ones I had when I graduated from college. I also learned I'm not making the progress I'd like to make. So, I asked myself, 'What would the third brother do?' Several questions immediately came to mind: Who are the experts I can study? What's the best way to set my goals? And what's the best way to accomplish my goals?"

Brad slowly answered. "Great questions. Did you find answers?"

"I sure did. Searching for experts to study, I found the late Paul Meyer. He's the founder of Success Motivation Institute and was quoted as saying, 'If you are not making the progress that you would like to make and are capable of making, it is simply because your goals are not clearly defined.' Learning that fact reminded me that one of the greatest things about America is our freedom to pursue goals. Many countries don't allow their people the freedom to set goals. In America, we can control the direction of our lives.

"Another article I found reminded me that even in America, most people are wandering generalities. They operate under the principle of Mutual Mystification."

"Mutual Mystification?" Brad interrupted.

"Yes, that happens when I don't tell you my goals, and you don't tell me what you expect; then, when I don't accomplish anything, neither of us is disappointed."

Brad laughed as he shook his head. "I've seen that behavior—just never knew it had such a great name… Mutual Mystification… I like it."

Joe continued, "I found another quote from Will Rogers who said, 'If you don't set your goals, the government will set them for you… which is OK if you want the government to run your life for you!' He also said, 'Thank God we don't get all the government we pay for.' And that was back in the 1920s."

"Wise man," Brad said.

Looking down, shaking his head, and then turning back to Brad, Joe said, "My goals until yesterday weren't clearly defined. Meyer suggested writing goals so clearly, you'll be able to vividly see them in your mind's eye. He also suggested setting long-range and short-range goals in seven important areas of life."

Joe pulled the folder back in front of him and took out seven new cards, each with a different title at the top: Physical, Social, Mental, Spiritual, Financial, Family, and Vocation. "I now have seven cards, Brad. Each is written on two sides. I wrote between two and five short-range goals on the front and between two and five long-range goals on the back. It took the better part of an hour, and I now have a total of about fifty goals."

Brad flipped through the cards and said, "Fifty goals? Sounds daunting! How did you feel after writing all this down?"

Joe's face brightened as he responded, "At first, it *was* daunting! But the more I worked on it, the easier and more exciting it became. I also found several articles that said goals have to pass what's called a SMART test, but the articles didn't explain what that is."

Brad smiled broadly, shaking his head in amazement. "Your third-brother timing is incredible." He reached into his pocket, pulled out the Action Step #3 card, and read it out loud.

Third-Brother Action Step #3

Make Your Goals "SMART"

Specific
Measureable
Achievable
Result-Oriented
Time-Framed

Then, as he slid it across the table, Joe interrupted. "Brad, great minds tend to think alike. Thanks for the card, but I haven't finished. Even though the articles didn't *specifically* define SMART goals, I knew you'd expect me to be the third brother, so I continued researching. Here's what I found.

"Specific means it's a goal I can visualize in my mind's eye.

"I can already see myself in the top four percent of salespeople in my company, so my goal for this program is specific.

"Measurable means just what it says. An example of a *non*-measurable goal might be… 'get better sales.' A measurable goal would be… 'close $50,000 in sales this month.'

"Achievable means I believe in my heart it's possible. I could set a goal to have ten million dollars by tomorrow morning, and I could *say* it's possible. But it's *not* something I would believe in my heart. Brad, I must believe in my heart that a goal is achievable for me to give it my best effort.

"Next, it must be Result-oriented, which means that someday I can mark it *done*—there's a specific deadline or ending. When you told me about your training program, you said it had a specific finish line, right?"

"Correct," Brad acknowledged. "A total of seventeen days."

"You know, Brad, the fact that this program is only seventeen days long made it possible for me to see the finish line from the start. That's probably one of the reasons I've been so motivated to do my daily assignments."

Joe continued. "And that leads to T—the final letter in SMART. A well-written goal must have a *Time-frame*. Shorter goals might be as-soon-as-possible while others a bit longer. And some, like earning a college degree, can take years. But every well-written goal needs a specific target date. So, I added realistic target dates for each of my new goals. Those targets added extra excitement and motivation to the goal-setting process.

"Brad, I went back and polished my goals to make sure each passed the SMART test. Doing this with each goal got me even more excited. You asked how I felt after writing down all those goals. Well, it's hard to explain. All I can say is, it felt like I was wandering through the desert, and someone suddenly handed me a glass of cold water. What started as a boring, daunting, and energy-draining exercise became a living document that generated excitement and actually created additional energy.

"Now, I have about fifty goals with more clarity than I can ever remember. I have enthusiasm and hope for the future. I can feel my increased energy. The goals aren't daunting, Brad. The uncertainty I felt *before* setting goals—that was the daunting part."

"Sounds like you learned a valuable lesson, Joe."

"There's even more." Joe said excitedly. "I continued researching and found one of the world's greatest goal-setters. His name is John Goddard. Around 1940, he wrote a list of 127 lifetime goals and called it his 'Life List.' These weren't simple or easy goals. They included climbing the world's major mountains, exploring the length of the world's longest rivers, piloting the world's fastest aircraft, running a mile in under five minutes, and reading the entire *Encyclopedia Britannica*. According to his home page, johngoddard.info, he accomplished 109 of those goals during his lifetime, and many more that weren't on his original list."

"So, your research into Paul Meyer, Will Rogers, and John Goddard taught you how to set and accomplish goals?"

"Not exactly!" Joe confessed. "I learned how to *set* goals, and I feel great when I look at them. But none of my research revealed how to *accomplish* them."

"So, you were *trained* without being *trained*. They trained you to *set* goals, but you're not trained to *accomplish* them, right?"

Pausing—with a blank expression—Joe answered, "You sure know how to rain on a parade!"

Both laughed. Then Brad said, "Now you're starting to see why most training programs don't work. Peter Drucker, who was a world-famous management consultant, said it best: 'Plans are only good intentions unless they immediately degenerate into hard work.' Let's talk about how to plan and *accomplish* your goals. This should take less than ten minutes."

"Wait a second, Brad. You're saying in less than ten minutes, you can train me on a process I can follow to accomplish my goals?"

"That's exactly what I'm saying," Brad stated. "It may take years to reach some goals, but I can train you in the step-by-step process in about ten minutes. You've already done the hard part—you started. Then you organized your goals in a logical way—into seven categories. Then you tested them to make sure they were SMART. By the way, Joe, that SMART principle has been around for years. But now, like the third brother, you're training yourself to 'smarten' *your* goals."

Brad paused. "Are you ready for the next step?"

"Fire away. I'm ready to tackle my next assignment."

"Here's the step-by-step procedure. It took us several years to develop and *prove* this process, but you can implement it *immediately*. Much like setting goals, accomplishing them will initially feel daunting. However, if you follow our procedure, you'll succeed. It may take a little while for it to become habitual, but it will, and then it will be easier and even fun. Our company's experience has proven there's no better step-by-step procedure anywhere for accomplishing goals."

Brad took five new cards and spread them left to right in front of Joe—Third-Brother Action Steps 4, 5, 6, 7, and 8. Then, starting with the first card on the far left, he led Joe through the cards, one at a time. He started by reading the first card out loud…

Third-Brother Action Step #4

Set Lifetime Goals

DAY 3: KNOWING YOUR PERSONAL AND PROFESSIONAL LIFETIME GOALS

"Joe, there are five parts to the procedure for accomplishing goals. You've already completed the first part. You've written down all the goals you want to accomplish. You listed your lifetime goals. You broke them into seven fundamental areas. You applied the SMART criteria. You separated them into long-range and short-range goals. Now, the challenge is to prioritize them and start working on the most important goals."

Tapping the second card, Brad read it out loud...

Third-Brother Action Step #5

Update Lifetime Goals Annually

Brad looked up from the card, and said, "Each year during the five days between Christmas and New Year's Eve, rethink, reprioritize, and rewrite your lifetime goals. As you do, keep the following points in mind.

"Your annual update is a critical step. That's when you decide which of your lifetime goals you'll accomplish in the coming twelve months. You can also plan additional goals that might not be as big as *lifetime*, but are important nonetheless! For example, you might have a lifetime goal to run the Boston Marathon, but your goal for the coming year could be to qualify. Or, if you haven't been training, your goal might be to complete a 10K race this year without walking and qualify *next year* for the Boston Marathon.

"The annual update is the time to ask yourself about adding new goals and maybe even eliminating others. It's also the time to ask yourself if some of your goals should have more than one level of accomplishment. For example, you might have a realistic goal to add $4 million in new sales in the next twelve months, but now add a dream goal of $5 million. Having a realistic goal and a dream goal in the same area can add fun and excitement to the process.

"You might also want to have more than one level of success in certain types of annual goals, such as running the Boston Marathon. You may have a minimum goal to just finish, along with a mid-level goal to cross the line in three and a half hours—and a dream goal of a top-3 Podium Finish in your age group.

Selecting the third card, Brad read it out loud…

Third-Brother Action Step #6

Update Annual Goals Monthly

"Starting December thirty-first, and continuing on the last Friday or Saturday of each month, ask yourself, 'What progress can I make toward my top priority goals in the next thirty days?' Make notes and create a list of your top-ten 'To-Dos' for the coming month."

Tapping the fourth card, Brad read…

DAY 3: KNOWING YOUR PERSONAL AND PROFESSIONAL LIFETIME GOALS

Third-Brother Action Step #7

Update Monthly Goals Weekly

"Using your monthly top-ten To-Do list, add the highest priority items to your calendar for the coming week. Polish your list and repeat this step each Friday."

Brad added, "If any single 'To-Do' on your list will take longer than two hours to complete, break it into smaller, more manageable chunks. All lifetime goals are accomplished one or two hours at a time. If things get tough, think of Sir Edmund Hillary. He climbed Mount Everest— one step at a time!"

Pointing to the fifth card, Brad read…

Third-Brother Action Step #8

During your weekly progress review, ask yourself what headway you can make in the coming week toward your most important goals.

"For the balance of the year, on the last Friday or Saturday of each month, review your progress and ask yourself what headway you can make in the next month toward your most important goals. Then each year between Christmas and New Year's, review, and if possible, improve your lifetime goals."

Brad raised his eyebrows and asked, "Any questions?"

"What you're saying is, I need to update my lifetime goals annually, update my annual goals monthly, and update my monthly goals weekly. It sounds complicated, but when I see it written out, it looks simple."

"It *is* simple!" It takes time and effort initially, but once you develop the habit, you'll find this step-by-step procedure saves more time than it takes. We'll talk more about accomplishing your goals as we go through the balance of the program."

Brad stood. "Your assignment for tomorrow is to pick one of your top short-range goals and work on that goal today for at least thirty minutes. Tomorrow, let me know what you learn."

Brad handed Joe another card. "Tomorrow, Joe, if we have time," Brad winked, "We'll talk about time management."

Joe read the card slowly to himself as Brad walked to the counter to pay for their coffee.

Third-Brother Action Step #9

Manage the activities you do in the time you have available!

Time management is a waste of time!
You can't manage time!
The key is activity management.

As Brad walked out the door, Joe slowly read the card again, this time out loud, but softly. "Manage the activities you do… in the time you have available… Time Management is a waste of time! You can't manage time! The key is Activity Management… "

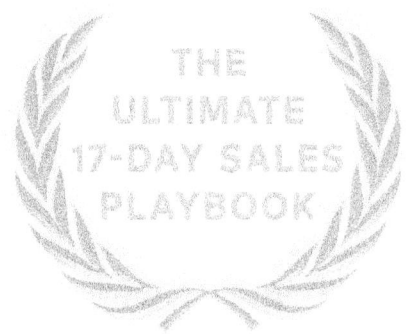

THE
ULTIMATE
17-DAY SALES
PLAYBOOK

Day 4: Replacing Time Management

5:30 a.m.

It was a rainy Saturday morning. Joe pulled up to the diner and stared through the rain-covered windows at the people inside. He let out a deep breath, not wanting to exit his car. Even though he felt better than when he first met Brad, he was still apprehensive about his future and wondered if he could really become a good salesperson. He felt almost the same way he did before meeting Brad.

Doubts clouded his mind. He wondered… "What's the point of meeting each morning? I have no results to show for it. Setting my goals was great, but when I woke up this morning, I realized they're possibly out of reach. I would probably be better off getting more sleep and being fresh for work on Monday."

Still, he slowly entered the diner. Approaching Brad, he faked a smile. His 'good morning' to Brad sounded insincere.

Brad frowned. "Maybe for me, but it doesn't seem like a good morning for you. Is everything okay?"

Sliding into the booth, Joe answered, "It's early, but I'm fine and ready to go."

"No," Brad insisted. "How are you, really?"

"Brad, I'm tired. It's Saturday. I appreciate what you're doing, but I'm concerned about my progress. Our meetings remind me of when people come back from a conference or a seminar. They're excited at first, and they *say* they're committed, but nothing seems to change. I was excited and committed, but I think I got caught up in the moment these last few days. Now I'm feeling no different, and nothing appears to be changing."

Brad didn't seem surprised at Joe's frustration. "Joe, you showed up. That's eighty percent of the battle, and I commend you for it. This program isn't for everyone—only those committed to being part of the top four percent. You can quit at any time. Like I said a couple of days ago, once you start, quitting is the only way to fail… Is that what you want to do?"

Joe glanced down and then back at Brad but didn't answer. His silence said it all.

Brad continued. "When we first met, I told you about a way you could change your habits—a way to get into the top four percent. You got excited! You committed to the work! And *I* committed to show you the way.

"I'm not going to pull any punches, Joe. From here on, there's a lot of work—maybe an extra hour or two every day. Remember, you're already on Day 4, and you have less than two weeks to go. Quitting is always an option, but so is continuing. It's one day at a time."

Again, Joe looked down and then back at Brad, but this time he said, "Brad, I have to confess, I almost slept in this morning, but I would have felt bad if I stood you up. I just want to get better at my job!"

"Sleeping in is always an option, Joe. Many people go to work every day like they're sleeping, anyway. They're okay with the status quo, and they just go through the motions. If you only want to get better at your job—next week, double your cold-call count and ask your current customers for more business. Work harder! You'll likely get better results."

Joe's eyes opened wide as he interrupted, "You could have told me that the first day we met."

Brad raised his eyebrows. "I didn't say it because it won't get you into the top four percent. Working harder will help a lot of people in the bottom 96 percent, but it's not the key to getting into the top four percent!"

"Then what *is* the key?" Joe asked.

DAY 4: REPLACING TIME MANAGEMENT

"You've heard the old cliché, 'Work smarter, not harder.' Well, that's not the answer either! The real key is a balanced approach to working smarter *and* harder.

"We still have a few days to build our foundation. So, what do you say? Are you ready for today's session?"

Joe nodded. "I'm glad you haven't given up on me."

Brad signaled for the server to bring Joe's coffee. "My apology, Joe. I should have had that waiting when you arrived." Then he asked, "What did you learn yesterday?"

Joe opened his folder. Then, looking up, said, "You asked me to pick a goal that could be done quickly and work on it for thirty minutes. This assignment was a big part of my frustration. The goal I chose was to make five cold calls by phone in a half hour. I made the calls, but it took over an hour. I ended up late for a meeting with a client."

"Why did it take more than an hour?" Brad asked.

"Three of the calls went straight to voice mail, but the other two resulted in appointments. I was only on the telephone for ten minutes with each of the two good calls, but the follow-up emails and planning ran me well over the original thirty minutes. It was exciting and good—but also exasperating."

Brad smiled, acknowledging Joe's frustration. "Lesson learned—welcome to the world of poor time management."

"Wait a minute," Joe said. "If there's poor time management, there must also be good time management, right?"

Brad laughed softly, "No, Joe. All attempts to manage time are bad. Read your Action Step #9 card again."

Joe opened his folder, looked at the card, and read, "Third-brother action step number nine… manage the activities you do in the time you have available. Time management is a waste of time. You can't manage time. The key is activity management."

He looked up. "So, where did I go wrong?"

"Joe, your goal was *smart*, and your execution was excellent. But your planning was faulty. You didn't anticipate the interruptions you would encounter, and you didn't plan for the extra actions you would need to take. It was your *activity* management that caused you to miss your appointment."

Still frustrated, Joe asked, "So, how *should* I have planned?"

Brad answered, "It's difficult to predict how much time it will take to accomplish certain tasks, and it's impossible to predict interruptions. Since we don't know for sure how much time they'll take, we need a system that's flexible... but still effective.

"From now on, when you plan a job or a goal, it's essential to add blocks of time to your schedule to allow for unplanned activities and interruptions. The name we gave to this flexible and effective planning system is *Time Blocking*."

"Time Blocking?" Joe responded; a bit confused.

Brad nodded, "Correct! It's a technique used by everyone in the top four percent. Time Blocking is reserving blocks of time or appointments on your calendar for all activities needed to accomplish your goals. Some of these blocks or appointments will be with clients, some with prospects, some with yourself, and some empty or blank time blocks will be for contingencies and flexibility.

"The top four percent schedule specific blocks of time for appointments, prospecting, cold calling, assigned tasks, goals, planning, and *especially* empty blocks of time for flexibility. They create an average of thirty to sixty of these time blocks on their calendars each week. Each block can be a half hour, full hour, or even two hours, and the blocks are different each week. They put these appointments on their calendar. That is, they reserve these blocks of time, so they'll have time to do the activities needed for their goals, responsibilities, and commitments, as well as interruptions and other contingencies."

"Brad! That was a mouthful. You're saying the top four percent treat their time blocks as hard appointments—even when the time-blocked appointments are with *themselves*?"

Brad nodded as he answered, "That's right! The top four percent typically plan five to ten time blocks each week for making phone calls to set and manage appointments. They schedule an additional five to ten time blocks every week for sales calls with prospects and clients. And they reserve twenty—or more—empty time blocks for the other contingencies we just mentioned.

"Another thing, Joe. When you're setting appointments, it's important to stay in control of your calendar. When you start time blocking your calendar, try not to block more than half of your week. You'll need some unblocked time to allow for unplanned travel, administrative duties, unexpected opportunities, or problems. Also, when setting an appointment with a prospect or client, always suggest one or two times that correspond with your preplanned time blocks. Never ask, 'What's good for you?' When you ask that question, you're giving control of your calendar to another person. It may be polite, but it's not the most effective way to manage your schedule.

"Joe, good activity management has four distinct steps: goal setting, planning, organizing, and—the most important—executing.

"Goal setting is the foundation. If you don't have goals, you don't need planning, and you won't need organization or execution because you're not going anywhere! Your goal was to make five cold calls in one thirty-minute time block. However, you didn't plan your calls in a way that allowed for the unexpected.

"You should have scheduled an additional thirty to sixty-minute time block immediately following your thirty-minute cold-call time block as a buffer time block for follow-up, and for the unexpected interruptions.

"Your organization was good, and your execution was excellent, but your planning error created frustration.

"Now listen carefully! Let's review the four important things you need to do to best manage your activities. First, decide what *smart* annual goals you want to accomplish. Then, break your annual goals into monthly goals. For example, if you want to sell $5 million in one year, you might break that goal into $500,000 per month increments. That way, you're actually aiming at $6 million for the year, and you have a little buffer each month in case you miss one or more of your monthly goals. Each month, break your monthly goals into weekly goals. Then each week, break your weekly goals into smaller half-hour to two-hour daily goals… time blocks! These are the weekly building blocks for your monthly, yearly, and lifetime achievements.

"The second thing to do to best manage your activities is to plan your coming week by checking your calendar for scheduled commitments, like meetings and appointments. During the uncommitted portions of each day, reserve time blocks for your smaller half-hour to two-hour daily goals. Be sure to include time blocks for goal setting and planning, as well as travel and other contingencies like interruptions or unexpected opportunities—these are the appointments with yourself that we talked about earlier.

"If anyone hits you with 'Got a minute?' or schedules a meeting that conflicts with a planned time block, politely decline if possible. Let them know you have a commitment for that time. Suggest another time that fits your calendar—one that might also fit theirs.

"The third thing is to organize the resources necessary to accomplish your plan. What agendas, samples, brochures, testimonials, proposals, or other things will you need? These tend to be the things that are overlooked or not addressed until the last minute by the bottom 96 percent.

"The fourth thing in managing your activities is execution. Goal setting, planning, and organization are a waste of time if you don't execute. Execution will be the focus for the balance of our program.

"Now, for your assignment… "

Brad slid two cards over to Joe. Then, as Joe picked up the cards, Brad recited the first card from memory. "Time management, which is really activity management, is like a building with four floors. The lower foundation level is titled Goals. The second level is Plans. The third is Organize, and the top level is Execute."

Third-Brother Action Step #10

Then he read the second card:

Third-Brother Action Step #11

Build from the ground up... one block at a time!

1. Set your goals
2. Develop your plan to accomplish them
3. Organize your resources
4. Execute your plan
5. Review progress, and repeat until complete

"Joe, I want you to take one of your top priority goals in one of the seven areas you mentioned on Day 3. Then build a four-story building for that goal and bring it back Monday morning. Start with one of your highest priority short-range goals—break it into manageable, less than two-hour chunks—then time-block the chunks that you will do next week. You can work on the other six goal areas later."

Joe nodded, confirming his understanding of Brad's assignment. Brad then stood and asked, "Same time Monday?"

Joe was concerned. "Brad, can we meet tomorrow to review how I should plan my week? Maybe you could show me how you plan yours."

Brad hesitated before replying. "Joe, Sundays are for my family. However, I like that you want to be prepared with your goals and plans, and I want you to be ready to execute on Monday morning. So, yes… I'm willing to meet tomorrow. But let's make it eight o'clock rather than five-thirty."

As Brad took a step to leave, Joe pulled the check from his mentor's hand. "My treat today, and besides, I'm going to stay awhile to get a good start on my assignment."

Brad nodded his appreciation, then turned and headed out the door.

Sunday Progress Review

8:00 a.m.

The sun was already up as both Joe and Brad walked into the diner at the same time. They exchanged a handshake. Brad wasn't as dressed up as on the other days, but he still looked sharp in a buttoned-down patterned shirt, jeans, polished shoes, and blazer.

Their usual booth was empty, and, like creatures of habit, they ordered their standard coffee. Clearly, their relationship was growing stronger as they felt comfortable with each other. Their mood felt casual.

"Thanks again for meeting today, Brad. I know Sunday is a day you spend with your family, so I especially appreciate your meeting this morning to share how you typically plan your week."

"Happy to help, Joe. And, yes, Sunday *is* a special day. I get to see my grandkids where my wife and I attend church, and then they usually come over for lunch. I always look forward to Sunday. Those grandkids help me keep a balanced perspective on life!"

Brad took a sip of coffee and leaned back, looking relaxed. "Joe, you asked to meet today so I could show you how I plan my week. Well, I start by spending time with my family on Sunday. Like I said on Day 2 of our program, they're the reason I work. I also do something every weekend that's a critical activity for the coming week. Every Saturday or Sunday evening, I plan a one-hour time block to reflect on the past week and plan the next. I'll share what I do during that hour—but first, let me give you an illustration.

"Imagine you have an empty, one-gallon glass beaker in front of you. Your beaker represents the coming week, and you want it to be as full as possible. You start filling it with large rocks one by one until it's full to the top. You look at it, notice a few gaps between the rocks, and ask, 'How can I get more into my jar?'

"More large rocks won't fit, so you pick up pebbles and drop them in. They cascade down and nestle in around the larger rocks until the jar is clearly full. Then you ask, 'Can I fit any more into the jar?'

"You can still see small empty spaces, so you add sand and shake the jar a little to ensure the sand settles around the pebbles and large rocks.

"The jar looks full, but you take a pitcher of water and pour it into the beaker. It fills in around the large rocks, pebbles, and sand until it reaches the top. Now, Joe, can you fit in anything else?"

"This must be another trick question, Brad."

The older man laughed and said, "Not a trick. The jar is as full as it will get. So let me ask you, what's the point of this illustration?"

Joe thought for a moment, then slowly responded, "I guess no matter how full it seems, there's always room for more."

"That's what everyone thinks, but no! The illustration teaches us to put the big rocks in first, or they'll never fit. Can you see how this might apply to your weekly planning?"

Joe scratched his head as Brad continued, "If you fill the jar with water, sand, and pebbles at the start, you'll have no space left for the large rocks. Does that help you see why it's important to time-block your big goals while you still have room on your calendar?"

Joe paused, then smiled. "Yeah… I can see that now."

Brad continued, "Most people wrongly confuse being busy with being productive. The pebbles, sand, and water represent busy work. The big rocks represent productivity.

"Joe, I use my weekend time block to see where I am—decide where I want to go in the coming week, and then build a bridge to cross the gap. I do this by first asking myself seven questions and time blocking as many big rocks as possible into my coming week."

Brad pulled two new cards from his inside jacket pocket. "I planned to give you these on Monday, but they're relevant for today. These are the seven questions I ask myself each weekend." Brad then read the first card out loud.

Third-Brother Action Step #12

Answer these questions each weekend

1. What are my top big-rock personal goals this week?
2. What are my top big-rock work goals this week?
3. What opportunities exist for me to make progress?
4. What obstacles do I anticipate?
5. What are current best solutions to these obstacles?
6. Who can I ask for help?
7. How many time-blocks must I invest?

"Answering those seven questions, Joe, will help you identify and plan the activities required to accomplish your goals. Then, each day at the end of the day, review where you are versus where you want to go and adjust the next day's calendar if needed."

Brad picked the second card and said, "This is very much like Action Step #10, except it is specifically for this week's goals." Brad then read the second card out loud.

> # Third-Brother Action Step #13
>
> ## *Time-block one hour on Friday, Saturday, or Sunday to plan your coming week*
>
> **Review** this week's "Big-rock" Goals
> **Plan...** Time-block the next seven days
> **Organize** resources and "to-do's"
> **Execute!**
>
> *(Be sure to include your personal goals!)*

"Joe, as I said yesterday, goal setting, planning, and organizing are a waste of time—if you don't execute! Remember, all four steps are essential, but the last step is critical!" He then asked his younger friend, "Joe, it's not yet due, but have you started your assignment for Monday?"

Joe nodded as he pushed his completed assignment across the table to Brad, obviously pleased that Brad had asked.

Brad donned his reading glasses and reviewed Joe's work. When he finished, he gazed over the top of his readers and said, "This is excellent! You looked at your week objectively and made decisions, and developed personal goals and work goals that are *smart*. You wrote them down—and that's the foundation of the building."

Looking up, Brad continued. "Your week has a clear path forward. You've broken your big-rock goal into smaller, more manageable chunks, and now you're ready to time-block the coming week. Tomorrow, bring your plan for the week. And remember to schedule those empty, 'buffer' time blocks we talked about yesterday to allow for flexibility in your work week—to allow for the unexpected, unplanned, and unknown!

"One more thing, Joe. The top four percent salespeople are especially good with the sixth question—asking for help from someone who's done it before. That alone can save months of execution. I want you to think through how I can help you achieve your goals this week. Thinking about how others can help is an important exercise… assuming you want significant growth; the kind of growth I believe you're capable of accomplishing.

"And by the way, I ask myself these same questions *every* weekend. Tonight, before my head hits the pillow, I will have next week planned, time-blocked, organized, and ready for execution. Joe, that sparkle in your eye tells me you're going to do the same."

"I will!" Joe nodded in agreement.

"One last thing for today. I'll repeat myself because this may be the most critical habit you'll ever develop. Tonight and every night hereafter, review your weekly plan and decide what you want to accomplish the next day. This exercise will initially take fifteen minutes to a half hour. But within two weeks, you should have it down to three to five minutes. Make this your daily exercise. At the end of each day, review your goals and, if necessary, adjust your plan for the next day."

Brad glanced at his watch, smiled, and scooted out of the booth.

"Tomorrow, I'll go deeper into Thought-Habit-Action Patterns. I first mentioned them on Day 1. We'll talk about how to program your mind to automatically make excellent decisions.

"Joe, I'm proud of the changes you've made. I'll see you early tomorrow morning. Until then, I have a church service to attend, some grandkids to enjoy, and later this evening, an hour time block I set aside to review my goals for the coming week. Those are *my* big rocks for today."

With that, Brad scooped up the bill, paid at the counter, and left the diner.

Joe stayed in the booth to think about his big rocks for the day and the coming week.

Day 5: Building Thought–Habit–Action Patterns

5:30 a.m.

Brad walked into the diner and spotted Joe already hard at work. He no longer appeared depressed or worried.

Joe was deep in thought and did not notice Brad approaching. Brad felt a sense of optimism as he tapped Joe on the shoulder. "Mind if I join you?"

Joe's eyes widened with enthusiasm. "Hey Brad, thanks again for meeting me yesterday. I worked on the assignment you gave me, and I even typed it up so you can review my progress. Consider it an executive briefing."

Brad sat across from Joe and placed his briefcase on the seat beside him.

"Before we begin, Brad, I want to sincerely thank you for your willingness to work with me. It means a lot, and I want you to know I appreciate you."

"It's my pleasure." Brad smiled, impressed with Joe's sincerity and diligence.

Joe continued, "I developed my first building and took a couple of smaller personal and work goals to plan the necessary time blocks I would need. Then I reorganized my calendar for the coming week, and now I'm ready to execute."

The server brought Joe a refill along with Brad's usual.

"I won't ask you what you learned this time. You're already demonstrating third-brother behavior. I'm seriously impressed. We're only on Day 5, so great job! Now let's move on to your next lesson.

"We've already touched on the importance of Thought-Habit-Action Patterns. They're our personal decision-making templates. These are things programmed into our brains that cause us to respond the way we do. And the good news is, we can reprogram ourselves to make consistently excellent decisions automatically."

Joe interrupted and said, "Glad you're bringing that up. I did some research on Thought-Habit-Action Patterns and was surprised to find a good explanation on the Internet."

"Really?" Brad smiled with one eye half-closed. "Did your research verify what they are and where they come from?"

"Yes," Joe said as he opened his notebook. "Thought-Habit-Action Patterns are just what the name implies. They're habitual patterns of thought that lead to predictable patterns of behavior. They're automatic responses to people, situations, and the world around us.

"We first *sense* things—we see, hear, touch, taste, and smell. Then what we sense, along with our responses and the subsequent results, are stored in our subconscious memory as internal programming. Second, we *associate* what we sense with our internal programming. Subconsciously, we ask ourselves, 'Have I seen this before?' Third, we *evaluate* what we're sensing by subconsciously comparing it with what we already know. And fourth, we *make decisions* that always cause mental activity and sometimes trigger physical actions.

"Brad, my research also surfaced information on you and your company, Allied Applied Sciences. I found a speech you gave at a Chamber of Commerce meeting over forty years ago. I copied those four steps from your speech."

Brad interrupted. "Joe, your research is excellent. When I gave that speech, it was right after I learned about Thought-Habit-Action Patterns. In fact, that's when my career and my life were transformed. My growth accelerated, and it was a significant factor that helped me break into the top four percent. It transformed my decision-making process and is still today transforming many of our people.

"But Joe, this isn't about me or my company. Let's get back to what you learned about Thought-Habit-Action Patterns and what you still need to learn in this program over the next twelve days. Those four steps help us understand why we respond to things and to others the way we do. Equally important, they help us understand why other people respond the way *they* do.

"Understanding your own—and other people's—Thought-Habit-Action Patterns will help you to better understand one of life's greatest secrets about the human mind. The secret is so simple it will transform you from a human *doing* into a human *being*."

Brad reached into his coat pocket, took out a card, and handed it to Joe as on the previous days. This time, however, it appeared incomplete.

Joe turned the card and read it out loud.

Third-Brother Action Step #14

Make automatic "Best" Decisions!

Mary had a little _____

Then he read the last line on the card again. "Mary had a little... *lamb?*"

Brad shook his head and pointed to the card. "No, Joe, it doesn't say that. It says, 'Mary had a little...' *You* added the word lamb. Tell me, did you have any choice in completing the sentence with 'lamb'?"

Joe looked up and shrugged.

"Okay." Brad continued. "Let me give you two more examples. When I say, 'Two plus two,' you immediately think 'four.' If I say, 'Santa Claus,' you immediately picture a man in a red suit with a white beard, right?"

Feeling somewhat confused, Joe asked, "OK, but what does this have to do with Thought-Habit-Action Patterns... and with sales?"

"All three of those examples are things you programmed—or allowed to be programmed—into your memory. All three responses are automatic, *and* each is the most appropriate response for what you initially sensed.

"Here's an interesting fact. There's an infinite number of answers to the question, 'How much is two plus two?' But, only *one* answer is correct—only *one* is most appropriate. By the time you're in the fourth grade, only one answer is automatic.

"There are millions of ways you could have completed the sentence: 'Mary had a little... '. You could have said 'brother,' 'sister,' 'problem,' 'hernia,' 'wart,' et cetera, but you chose 'lamb.' Why?"

Joe's forehead wrinkled as he responded, "It was the first thing that popped into my head."

"Excellent! But you got it backwards. It was the first thing that popped *out* of your head. The word 'lamb' was already there! It had been programmed into your brain long ago. Today, when 'Mary had a little' hits your brain, the thought creates a habit-action pattern, and you automatically think 'lamb'!

"Listen carefully, Joe. This part is critical! Like I said, there are millions of ways you could have completed 'Mary had a little...'. But there was only one automatic and most appropriate—only one 'best' response. So, from now on, we are defining the word 'lamb' to mean *an automatic, most appropriate response.*

Brad leaned forward. "What we discovered forty years ago is that those lambs—as we just defined them—are another key to getting into the top four percent. We discovered the best way to succeed in selling is to have a lamb for every situation we might face."

Joe shook his head in confusion. "Doesn't it depend on the situation? And how do you develop lambs for millions of things people can say or do? How do you develop a lamb for every objection you might hear?"

"Those are exactly the questions we had forty years ago," Brad responded. "But when we made a list of all the objections that we had ever heard in selling or in persuading people to do something, we were shocked at how few there actually are! In fact, there are less than thirty! Now, assuming this is true, and assuming there will always be one best, most appropriate response for each objection, how many lambs will you need to answer every objection in selling? Or, for that matter, how many lambs will you need for answering objections any time you are trying to persuade others to do anything?"

Joe guessed, "Less than thirty?"

Joe's confused expression made Brad chuckle. "You're correct; you'll need fewer than thirty. Just as there are a million ways to answer, 'Mary had a little…' but only one *best* answer, so there are a million ways to answer the objection, 'Your price is too high.' And there are a million ways to respond to 'I want to think it over.' In fact, there are millions of ways to respond to every objection. But for *each* objection, there will only be *one… best* way!

"We'll cover lambs in more detail in a couple of days after we complete your top four percent training foundation. But for now, let's summarize where we are with Thought-Habit-Action Patterns.

"This is important, so I'm going to repeat what you just said… It's what you found in that old speech I gave years ago. The *whole*

Thought-Habit-Action Pattern process is best understood by breaking it into four steps.

"Like you said, first we *sense* something. Second, we *associate* it with our current internal programming. Third, we *evaluate* or interpret what's happening based on our internal programming. And fourth, we make a decision. That decision is our response to what we sensed. It may not include a physical response, but it *will* always include a mental response.

"What we call 'thinking' is really the internal process that goes on when the things we're sensing are being processed by our internal subconscious programming. For most people, their Thought-Habit-Action Patterns respond so quickly they often say or do things they regret.

"Now listen carefully, Joe. The quality of our decisions will be determined by the quality of our internal programming.

"The new and old programming combine to control our immediate decisions—our immediate responses! Your challenge is to train your brain to *always* make great decisions. That's what the balance of this program will do.

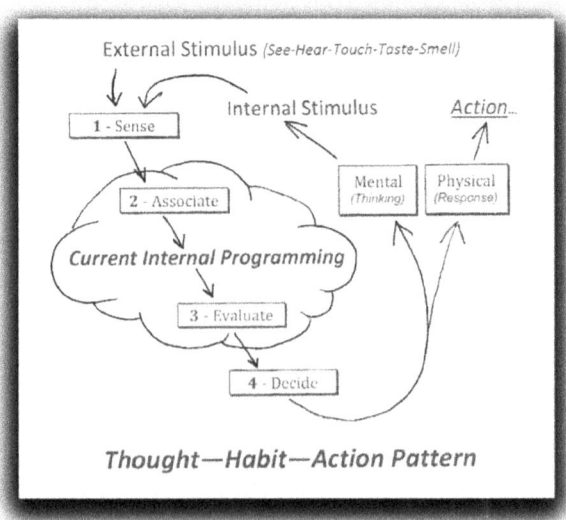

"Basic brain training is automatic. It starts when you are born and continues until you die. Your brain is always on—always training itself! As long as you are alive, you can't turn it off. Recently, I read a book by Randy Alcorn, titled *Heaven*. He claims we will even be learning new things after we die. But that's a whole different subject. Back to Thought-Habit-Action Patterns.

"Every day, your brain gets bombarded with sensory input—with external and internal stimuli. Some you control—and much you do not! Some are good, some are bad, and some don't seem to matter. You have little choice about much of this sensory input, but you do get to choose how you respond! Maturity and wisdom come from the choices you make after receiving sensory input. You must choose to program mature and wise responses to internal and external stimuli. These mature and wise responses will then become your automatic, best responses—your Thought-Habit-Action Patterns.

"Simply put, Joe, you are *programming* your brain to make wise decisions. It's what training is all about!

"Now, for your next assignment, I want you to do three things. The first will only take about five minutes. Make a list of *all* the objections you have ever heard or think you might hear. Objections are reasons—or justifications—prospects give for not buying. Typical objections are 'Your price is too high,' 'I want to think it over,' 'I need to get more bids.' Don't be surprised, Joe, if you can only think of ten to fifteen objections. Most people initially think there are millions, and that's why they never attempt to list them. There may be millions of slight variations, but when you list them, you'll find there aren't that many real objections. Try not to include redundant objections."

Joe interrupted, "Redundant? What do you mean by 'redundant'?"

"Sometimes, Joe, you'll hear prospects say, 'Your price is too high.' Other times, you'll hear, 'I don't have the budget.' And you might even hear, 'I've got a friend in the business who can give me a much better price.' These three objections are redundant. They're all the same objection but stated differently. Basically, they're all saying the same thing—'your price is too high.' Once you recognize the redundancy—and build a good lamb for the basic price objection—you'll have a lamb that will work for *all* the redundant variations."

Joe still looked confused, so Brad continued, "Let me give you an example. Each of the price objections I just mentioned can be addressed with the same lamb. Any time you hear a price objection, no matter what form it takes, you can address the objection with the same lamb. Acknowledge the objection, convert it into a question, and then probe to find or clarify their concerns and their needs.

"Here's an example of a good price objection lamb. 'I don't blame you for not wanting to spend too much—do you have a budget in mind that you're trying to hit?' Then continue to probe until you're able to move forward with the sale. That lamb fits all three price objections, and it will likely fit every price objection you'll ever hear."

Joe nodded slowly, reflecting on this simple truth as Brad finished his coffee.

"The second part of your assignment will take twenty to thirty minutes. After listing every objection you have ever heard—or think you might hear—review your list and eliminate any obvious redundancies. Then write your current 'best' response—or lamb—for each objection on your list.

"In about a week, when we reach Day 12, we'll refine and polish both lists—your objections *and* your lambs. We'll finalize the best lambs for each of the objections at that time. For now, just list all the objections you can think of, along with your best response to each."

Joe looked up in surprise. "So the first two parts of today's assignment aren't due until Day 12?"

Brad nodded. "Each day between now and Day 12, review your list of objections and your corresponding best responses—your current *best* lambs—and polish your lists. As you think about these two lists over the next week, you'll gain a clarity that's hard to explain. You'll gain confidence in the quality and completeness of your list and responses. Also, don't be surprised if your list gets shorter as you recognize and eliminate redundancies."

Brad pulled another card from his jacket pocket. "The third part of your assignment is to fill in the blank on this card." Brad then read:

Third-Brother Action Step #15

Develop the most critical skill!

The most critical skill in selling is:

_____

Handing the card to Joe, Brad continued, "Joe, I want you to fill in the blank with what you believe is the most critical skill in selling. It's an easy answer, but most salespeople miss it. Think about it and let's see if we agree on the answer when we meet tomorrow."

Joe glanced at the card again, then smiled and looked back at Brad. "Another trick question?"

Brad stood to leave. "No trick, Joe. If you're going to develop the most critical skill, you have to know what it is! I'll see you tomorrow morning."

Brad shook Joe's hand and walked out of the diner.

THE
ULTIMATE
17-DAY SALES
PLAYBOOK

Day 6: Developing the Most Critical Skill

5:30 a.m.

Joe pulled into a parking space and was surprised to see Brad sitting on a bench just outside the entrance. The "Open" sign flashed above the door.

As Joe approached, Brad stood and greeted him. "Morning, Joe. Are we ready to go inside and get to work?"

A bit puzzled, Joe responded, "Yes, but we always meet inside. Why are you waiting out here?"

"Fair question. Why do you think?"

Caught off guard by Brad's question, Joe wasn't sure how to respond.

Brad opened the door, and they walked back to their customary booth. Again, Brad asked, "Joe, why do you think I was waiting outside?"

"I can only guess," Joe said. "Truthfully, I thought something might be wrong!"

"So, you don't *know* if anything's wrong. Why not?"

Joe stopped dead in his tracks. "*Brad,* you're confusing me!"

Both were seated as Brad signaled for their usual coffee. "The reason you don't know if anything's wrong is because you're not using the most critical skill in selling. Part of your assignment for today was to fill in the blank on the card I gave you. Did you do that?"

Joe pulled out the card and showed it to Brad.

"Joe! There's only *one* most critical skill, but you've written a bunch of answers on the card. One most critical skill is singular."

Chuckling nervously while Brad remained serious, Joe said, "There are many critical skills. How about persistence, listening, communication, planning, closing, and… "

Brad interrupted him. "But what is the *most* critical skill?"

Joe hesitated and then said, "I'm guessing the most critical skill is listening."

"Good guess," Brad said. "But totally wrong!" He took the Action Step #15 card from Joe and drew a big "X" almost from corner to corner. Handing it back, he said, "Keep this as a reminder of some important skills—even if it's *still* missing the most *important* skill.

"You think listening is the most important skill? Actually, Joe, my wife is one of the best listeners I've ever known. But I doubt she would succeed in selling even if she tried. First, she's not interested in a career as a salesperson, and second, listening is a critical skill but a distant number two behind the *most* critical skill.

"Let me tell a story that explains how I learned the most critical skill. Early in my career, I was a machine. No one made more cold calls than me. I was fearless. I was persistent. I would ask for the sale and thought I was doing a good job. But working as hard as I could, my results were never better than mediocre."

Joe interrupted, "I can identify with that!"

Brad continued, "One of my assigned accounts was a large hospital system. I knew I'd be a top producer if I could land even a small part of their business. I had a good rapport with the key decision-makers. Everyone there seemed to like me. They told me, 'Brad, you're a nice guy. You work hard. You're professional. We would work with you if you could service our equipment. But you don't have a government contract. All large orders must go out for bid, and we're only allowed to place large orders with authorized government contractors.'

"Obviously, calling on this account was frustrating. The cost for our company to become an authorized government contractor was enormous. For us to set up the internal systems, licensing, and independent audits, we needed over a quarter million dollars—*up front!* The company I worked for was small, and we didn't have that kind of money lying around.

"One day, our company announced a contest. Whoever brought in the most revenue during the contest period would win an all-expense paid trip for two to Las Vegas. Being recently engaged but essentially broke, I *really* wanted to win. I went on a cold-call spree in addition to visiting all my current accounts.

"Nothing changed. And when I called on that big hospital system, guess what?"

Joe raised his eyebrows as if to say, "Go on."

"The buyers reiterated what I already knew: We needed a government contract!

"However, Joe, this day ended differently. As I walked out feeling disheartened, one of the new buyers took pity on me and asked me to have a seat in her office. She asked what products I sold and why I hadn't sold anything there. I relayed my sad story about not having a government contract, and she asked why I kept dropping in if my company didn't have plans to get authorized as a government contractor. I told her I hadn't given up on getting the approval—that maybe one day things would change. She smiled at my naive tenacity, then went on to tell me that products and services costing less than $2,500 did not *need* to go through the normal government contracting system.

"Then she stood up and asked me to follow her. I followed her down a few hallways until she opened a storage room door. Inside were shelves full of products we could service. She asked if we could repair any of them for less than $2,500.

"She went on to say she would write an individual purchase order to our firm for each unit that could be repaired for less than $2,500. She added, 'If the repair for any unit is over $2,500, send it back, and we'll let it collect dust.'

"I walked out that day with more business than I had ever received. I won the trip, and shortly after, my new wife and I honeymooned in Las Vegas—all expenses paid! So, Joe, what's the most critical skill in selling?"

Joe thought for a second, then answered, "Luck?" He quickly sensed Brad was not amused. "Persistence? You never gave up. Or maybe focus. You really wanted to win the trip."

"You're right, Joe, I wanted to win the trip, but that's not *why* I won. Let me put the cookies on the bottom shelf. How does a man get engaged?"

Somewhat sheepishly, Joe responded, "He proposes?"

"Precisely! You don't magically get engaged. You ask a question! The most critical skill in selling is *asking questions.*

"Remember these four things, Joe. First, a question creates an obligation for the other person to speak. Second, a question creates an obligation for *you* to listen to their answers—listen to their *needs*. Do you remember when I said, 'For most people, their Thought-Habit-Action Patterns respond so quickly they often say or do things they regret'?"

Joe nodded.

"Well, questions create an obligation for you to *listen,* and there's less chance you'll say something you'll later regret!

"Third, questions help you accurately understand the other person's situation, and fourth, they help you to position your products and services as solutions to your prospect's needs. The ability to ask excellent questions is *the* most critical skill in selling—and in any other type of persuasion.

"The new buyer asked me questions to understand my situation. Then she was able to help me understand *her* situation and the opportunity that had always been there.

"If I had only asked the other buyers better questions when I first started calling on this account, I might have earned their business six months earlier. They even gave me major hints that I completely missed. Like when the buyers said all large orders must go out for bid, I should have asked, 'What about smaller orders?'"

Brad handed Joe a new card that looked the same as Action Step #15, but this card replaced the blank line with the correct answer: *Asking Questions.*

Third-Brother Action Step #16

Develop the most critical skill!

The most critical skill in selling is:
Asking Questions

"Keep your #15 card, Joe. The big 'X' I drew on your answers will remind you of the less important skills."

Joe looked at the card. "I guess I flunked that question."

"Most people do. Now let's look at the two basic types of questions—closed-ended and open-ended.

"First, closed-ended questions only require a yes-or-no answer, and they're excellent for gathering facts. However, open-ended questions require a more thoughtful, more complete answer. They're excellent for gathering opinions, feelings, and other information you'll need if you truly want to understand your prospect's situation. An example of a good closed-ended question is, 'Do you have a budget?' A good example of an open-ended question might be, 'Can you tell me how you determine your budget?' Or you could ask, 'Are others involved in the budgeting process?'

"Joe, most salespeople just talk… and talk… and talk. Great salespeople don't just talk! They communicate. They use a combination of open-ended and closed-ended questions to navigate the conversation and determine the prospect's real needs. They don't have to guess like you did when you arrived this morning."

"So, what did I do wrong?"

"When you drove up and asked why I was outside, I replied, 'Why do you think?' Then, you immediately started guessing.

"What if you had followed up with a question? You could have easily responded by asking, 'Is everything OK?' You would have found the reason sooner for my sitting outside, and that would have saved time.

"One more point to remember. It's not just about asking any question; it's about asking *good* questions. Good questions will catapult you into the top four percent." Brad pulled another card from his pocket that read:

Third-Brother Action Step #17

Ask and you shall receive!

**If you don't receive good answers,
ask better questions.**

DAY 6: DEVELOPING THE MOST CRITICAL SKILL

"Your assignment for tomorrow is to list at least ten strong, closed-ended questions. Then make another list of at least ten strong, open-ended questions. These questions should ask for information that will help you understand and verify your prospect's needs. In a few days, we'll be going much deeper into identifying prospects' needs, but for now, tomorrow's assignment is to create the two good lists of questions.

"One more thing, Joe. Yesterday we talked about objections. Part of your assignment was to make a list of all the objections or reasons people can give for not buying your products or services. How many objections did you come up with?"

Joe pulled a sheet of paper from his folder. He handed it to Brad. "It doesn't look like I worked on this part of the assignment, but I did! I came up with only twelve objections. I know there must be more."

Brad smiled. "Actually, the assignment was to list every objection you could think of, and you *did* that. There are millions of variations of objections. But if you blow away the smoke and combine redundant objections, you'll find there are only eight. We'll prove that on Day 12."

"I also said there can only be *one best response* to each objection. You were supposed to start working on your best responses. Did you do that?"

Joe raised his eyebrows, "You mean lambs, as in Mary had a little…?"

"Right you are," Brad said and then laughed. "That was a good *clarifying* question. Now, back to *my* question. Did you develop any *lambs*?"

Joe nodded. "I did!"

Brad gestured with a thumbs-up. "Excellent! We'll need your objections—*and* lambs—in a few days when we talk about *best* lambs. In the meantime, keep polishing your lists of objections *and* lambs.

"All these things will soon tie together, Joe—Thought-Habit-Action Patterns, goals, planning, questions, objections, and lambs. We'll link them in the next seven days, so buckle your seat belt. We're about to accelerate."

Joe took a deep breath and sighed. "It seems like we've already accelerated."

Brad hesitated, then asked, "Back on Day 1, we talked briefly about our Third-Brother Playbook. Do you remember?"

"Yes," Joe said. "And if anyone needs a playbook, it's me."

"Tomorrow, we'll start building yours. It will be your guide for the balance of the program—and I predict—for the rest of your career! Are you ready?"

"More than ready, Brad. Is there any reason you feel I'm *not* ready?"

Standing to leave, Brad answered, "Good question! You *are* ready! Keep up the excellent work, and I'll see you bright and early tomorrow morning."

"Brad, one final question… was there any other reason you were sitting outside other than to teach this lesson?"

"Maybe one."

Brad patted the pocket that held his little Bible. "I like people-watching and praying for them. You probably didn't notice me sitting in that same spot last week on the day we first met—but I noticed you."

Joe pondered Brad's words as Brad smiled, turned, and departed.

Day 7: Creating Your Personalized Third-Brother Playbook

5:30 a.m.

Joe hurried into the diner, eager to take the next step. Brad was sitting in their usual booth, reading his Bible; he glanced up, closed it, and set it aside.

Approaching their booth, Joe said, "Good morning." Then, as he was taking his seat, he nodded toward the small book. "Is that the playbook you mentioned yesterday?"

Smiling, Brad said, "No, it's a different kind of playbook. It's the Bible you saw me reading last week. Have you ever studied it?"

Joe felt a little discomfort, shifting in his seat. "Bits and pieces."

Brad tucked the Bible into his coat pocket. "I never really studied it either until one day, sitting right here in this diner, I prayed for God to show Himself—to show me if He was real."

Joe was surprised and asked: "What happened?"

Brad, shaking his head slowly, answered: "At that exact moment—well, nothing happened—not at first. But I started noticing articles about God and the Bible, and then I met a lot of people who asked me questions about what I believed. Over the course of several months, I found people and books that helped me understand what the Bible says.

"Once I got serious about studying Scripture, it came alive. I can't explain it to you, Joe, but if you ever want to study it, I'd love to help you—like others helped me."

Joe nodded and then quickly changed the direction of the conversation. He didn't want a sermon, so he asked, "What about selling? Did all that Bible stuff help you in selling?"

"It did." Brad's eyes brightened as he answered. "If there's ever anything I can do to help you understand the Bible, please don't hesitate to ask. But for now, let's get back to your assignment for today."

Feeling relieved to leave that discussion behind, Joe opened his folder.

"Did you make your lists of ten closed-ended and ten open-ended questions? And, by the way, that's a closed-ended question."

Feeling good about his completed assignment, Joe handed over several pages to Brad. "Yes, I did!"

Brad read through Joe's work. "These are good."

"Thanks!"

Brad finished reviewing Joe's questions, then looked up and said, "I notice you have three lists: one for closed-ended questions, one for open-ended, and one labeled miscellaneous. Why the third list?"

Joe glanced at the third list and then back at Brad. "Some closed-ended questions generate more than a yes-or-no response. They're the reason for the third list."

The look on Brad's face said, "Go on."

Joe took the miscellaneous sheet and said, "Here's an example, 'Do you have any questions that haven't yet been answered?' That is a closed-ended question. It can be answered with a yes or no. If the answer is no, you're ready to move on to the next step. But if the answer is yes, the other person will feel an obligation to explain—like an open-ended question. I'm not sure which list to use for questions like this."

With a pleased smile on his face, Brad replied, "Joe, you're doing more than I asked. You're turning into a *third brother*." Joe's shoulders relaxed.

After a brief pause, Brad continued. "Your additional miscellaneous questions are excellent, but as you said, they *are* closed-ended and should be kept with that list. If you think about it, Joe, all closed-ended questions can be answered with more than a yes or no, especially if you purposely hesitate to speak after you get a yes or no. Your hesitation communicates to the other person that you're waiting for a more expanded answer. We'll talk further about this in a few minutes. For now, keep all your questions in one of your two lists, and let's dive deeper into the differences between closed-ended and open-ended questions.

"As I mentioned yesterday, Joe, closed-ended questions typically only require a yes or no answer, and they're excellent for gathering facts. But open-ended questions require a more thoughtful answer and are excellent for learning other people's thoughts, motivations, feelings, and opinions. Some people believe you should only ask open-ended questions, but I don't agree. The top four percent salespeople move things forward with a mixture of both. However, when they're asking closed-ended questions, they seldom ask more than two in a row."

Joe interrupted. "Why is that?"

"If you ask more than two closed-ended questions in a row, it can start to feel like an interrogation instead of a conversation. Also, open-ended questions tend to be better for building relationships. They don't presume to have a fixed right or wrong answer. It's natural to feel less pressure when answering an open-ended question because there's less risk of being wrong when you're answering them." Brad paused. "Does all this make sense to you?"

"It does! And that was a great closed-ended question!"

Brad smiled back at Joe. "You're right—*and* you're wrong!"

Joe was puzzled. "Excuse me?"

"It was a closed-ended question, but it's one of the *worst!*"

"Okay, Brad, I've been asking the question, 'Does this make sense?' ever since I can remember. It helps me make sure I'm being understood. Now you're telling me it's a bad question?"

"Not just bad, Joe—it's *terrible!*"

Joe shook his head, knitting his brows together. "You're losing me."

"Let me explain, Joe. Have you ever asked people to do something and followed by asking, 'does that make sense?' or 'do you understand?' and they responded with a yes—only to learn later they did the *opposite* of what you asked?"

Joe looked concerned. "I guess I have. So, if asking 'Does this make sense?' is a bad question, what's a better question?"

Brad smiled widely. "Now that's an excellent open-ended question. What if I had asked my question this way: 'Would you paraphrase what you believe to be the difference between open-ended and closed-ended questions?'

"You see, Joe, your answer to 'Does this make sense?' *doesn't* confirm that you really understand. However, your answer to 'Would you paraphrase… ' *will* confirm if we're on the same page.

"When I asked the closed-ended question: 'Does that make sense?' it was like saying, 'I explained the difference perfectly, and since it was perfect, you obviously agree. Right?' It's *not* a good question!"

Joe looked down, shaking his head, "I can't believe how many times I've asked questions like that and wondered why prospects didn't buy."

"Joe, your first question was closed-ended and not good. And now, we've replaced it with an open-ended question that's much better."

"So, you're saying open-ended questions work better when you're selling something?"

"I'm saying it takes both, Joe. Good salespeople stimulate conversation with open-ended questions, and they solicit facts with closed-ended questions. Great salespeople tend to ask *more* open-ended questions to ensure understanding.

"Let's address your original concern and the reason for your third group of questions. These are, as I said, closed-ended questions, even though they often generate more than a yes or no. This is the reason, Joe, that it's critical—after *all* questions—to pause!

"Any time you ask a question, it's important to pause to give the other person an opportunity to think through and possibly expand their answers. Don't jump back into questioning until your prospect has responded and you have been silent for a few seconds. Allow them time to think—it encourages them to give a more complete answer.

Brad pulled out another card and slid it across the table to Joe, who read it out loud:

Third-Brother Action Step #18

Whether you ask a closed-ended question or an open-ended question, always wait for a complete answer!

Joe sighed and shook his head. "Wow, Brad, I can't believe how simple you make it."

"I didn't make it simple, Joe. It's *always* been simple. But to be honest, it took us thirty years to blow away the fog to reveal the simplicity. Now let's talk about where to safely store these questions so they'll be readily available when you need them."

Brad retrieved a three-ring vinyl binder from his briefcase. "Third-Brother Playbook" was handwritten on the cover.

Brad placed the binder in front of Joe and said, "Not everyone follows a playbook, Joe. Most people just wing it as they go through life. They drift along, hoping, praying, and looking for secrets to success or other shortcuts. The bottom 96 percent also stumble through years of sales calls without ever deciding how to plan a best sales call. They pride themselves on winging it and never experience the success that comes from great planning.

"It took years of trial and error to create this Third-Brother Playbook. Now I'm excited to share it with you. It's not a canned set of things we say or do—it's not a secret or a shortcut—it's the process we follow. And it hasn't changed much in the last ten years. Even so, we're still open—and looking—for ways to improve it."

Brad then lifted another binder from his briefcase. This one was leather, well-worn, and classy-looking. However, unlike Joe's almost empty new binder, this one seemed to be full and was about an inch thick.

"This is *my* playbook, Joe. I've been using it for the last forty years, but, like I said, it hasn't changed much in the last ten. I review it annually, polishing it wherever and whenever I can. And I still find myself using it as a resource before major presentations.

"We've found one of the characteristics of the top four percent salespeople is their commitment to continually review, polish, and follow their own personalized Third-Brother Playbook. They review the whole playbook as part of their annual planning. The top four percent go back to the basics each year to rethink, refine, and reinforce their foundation.

"Our foundation, Joe, is the Third-Brother Playbook. And now, it's yours as well."

"Are you saying this replaces my assignment folder—the one I've been bringing each day?"

Brad nodded, looking like a proud parent. "It does! We're replacing your folder with a binder. Everything we've talked about up to today—and all the assignments so far—have related to you personally, to your business, and to your goals. Each day from now on, you'll add new pages—new assignments—to your binder. You'll personalize your playbook as we continue through the seventeen-day program."

"Will this process work for others in my company?"

Brad quickly answered, "Yes and no! Yes, the process and the template will work for anyone who applies them properly. But no, the binder with your personal and professional goals, lambs, etc., will not work for others.

"What I'm saying is, the template might be the same for everyone, but customizing it for yourself is what makes it work. Your personalized playbook will be a growing repository of resources that will take you *to*—and keep you *in*—the top four percent."

Brad then asked, "Are you ready to put some meat on the bones?"

"More than ready," Joe responded enthusiastically.

"Before you flip through your new playbook, open it to the front page—the table of contents. It lays out seventeen days behind seventeen tabs. Each day in the program is like a porthole in a submarine. If one is ignored and left open, the boat may not sink, but it will create a negative morale factor inside the submarine. An open porthole will also reduce the performance and the likelihood of success. Joe, we know submarines don't have portholes, but do you know why I use portholes as an illustration?"

"Is it because every day in the program is important?"

"Excellent answer, Joe! Actually, excellent question! Now let's look at the tab dividers."

Joe read through the table of contents silently.

Third-Brother Playbook: Contents

Day 1 Starting the Journey
Day 2 Making Excellent Decisions Automatically
Day 3 Knowing Your Personal and Professional Lifetime Goals
Day 4 Replacing Time Management
Day 5 Building Thought–Habit–Action Patterns
Day 6 Developing the Most Critical Skill
Day 7 Creating Your Personalized Third-Brother Playbook
Day 8 Making the First Call on a New Contact
Day 9 Identifying Needs

Day 10 Qualifying—Finding the Real Needs
Day 11 Presenting
Day 12 Handling Objections
Day 13 Closing—Precipitating Action
Day 14 Measuring Quality
Day 15 Applying The Universal Law of Sales Success
Day 16 Completing the Challenge—What Now?
Day 17 Reaching True Top Four Percent Success

While Joe was reviewing the titles of each tab—each day in the full seventeen-day program—Brad said, "The good news is, you've already completed the first six days. Take the notes from your folder and put them behind the appropriate tabs. You can also put the lists of open-ended and closed-ended questions you created for today's assignment behind the tab for Day 6.

"When you look through your playbook, you'll find mostly blank pages. They're blank for a reason. I'll guide you, but you'll create each new page in your own playbook, personalizing it as you complete your daily assignments. Each day, we'll cover one of the remaining tabs. By Day 17, you'll have your playbook pretty much written. Keep doing your daily assignments, and I promise you'll have everything you need in your playbook to get into the top four percent."

"What goes behind the Day 7 tab?" Joe asked.

"That's what we're going to talk about now. We need to agree on a few definitions. These will go behind the Day 7 tab. Our first definition is for the word *sell*."

Warming his hands on both sides of his coffee mug, Brad said, "Most people have a distorted understanding of selling. Look up the word 'sell' in Webster's Dictionary, and you'll find definitions like *cheat... dupe... hoax... take advantage...* and many others. Roughly half of Webster's definitions of the word 'sell' paint a negative picture of selling. Why do you think that's so?"

Joe shrugged his shoulders and said, "I never thought about it."

"It's because it's true! Selling is generally disrespected as a profession—and for a good reason. Some salespeople routinely cross the ethics and honesty line, but the vast majority are good, hard-working, honest people who have never been trained.

"Again, I'm not saying they haven't had training; I'm saying they were never *trained*. Kind of like my little Border Terrier buddy, Gus." Brad shook his head, "I still can't believe he never spoke!

"Our definition of selling is quite different, Joe. It's the first of five definitions that help to form the foundation of our training program.

We define selling as finding people… who have needs… that our products and services can satisfy… and then filling those needs… in such a way that we—our customer *and* our company—*both* make a profit or a gain.

"This brings a whole new dynamic to selling. It introduces a new standard for the top four percent salespeople. Our definition adds the requirement that the prospect must profit or somehow make a gain. Our definition requires the salesperson to make sure each customer realizes a positive return on their investment.

"Our salespeople already know we will profit when they make a sale. But now they have an additional responsibility. Using our definition, salespeople have an ethical and moral responsibility to help their prospects—our future customers—to receive a positive return on *their* investment—a positive ROI. In other words, our way of selling requires both parties to benefit.

"Now, for a few more definitions."

Brad reached into his briefcase and pulled out a letter-sized page with the bold-faced word "Definitions" at the top. The word "selling" was the first definition on the page.

Brad Pointed to the top of the page, saying, "We just covered selling—our first definition. The second thing we want to define is 'Webster' selling. A few minutes ago, I mentioned some negative definitions of selling in the dictionary—cheat, dupe, hoax, etc. From now on, we will use Webster to describe the wrong way to sell. In the future, when I say that's a Webster technique, I'm saying don't do it; it's the wrong way—the salesperson wins, and the prospect loses. We don't want to cheat, dupe, or hoax anyone. It also means the salesperson doesn't care if the prospect realizes a positive ROI. We'll talk more about Webster selling when we get to Day 9.

"Let's look at three more definitions, then I want you to add this page to your playbook.

Brad then read the third definition. "Communication—various forms of human interactions where one person attempts to influence another to think, feel, do, say, be, or learn something different or new. Do you agree with this third definition?"

Staring at the definition for a few seconds, Joe shook his head no. "It sounds more like marketing than communication."

Brad laughed. "It does! That aside, do you agree with it?"

Joe shook his head again. "I'm not sure."

"Okay, maybe this will help… All forms of communication are designed to influence others. When you tell your spouse or parents or kids you love them, you're trying to influence them to feel something. When you tell your kids the importance of studying, you're trying to influence them to do their homework. When you explain to the officer why you were going so fast, you're trying to influence him or her to have mercy."

"When you put it that way, I suppose I agree."

"Excellent! Now here's the point, Joe: *Selling* and *communicating* are the same, with *one* major exception—in selling, the effectiveness of our communication is measured and reported—also known as the bottom line—and you're paid according to how well you do. This seventeen-day program is designed to train you to be more than just an excellent communicator; it's designed to train you to be an excellent persuader—an excellent salesperson!

Brad pointed to the fourth definition. "Persuasion—the right way to sell. It's the foundation of selling with integrity. It's influencing a person to think, feel, do, be, or learn something that will benefit them more than it will cost them.

"And the fifth definition on the page, Joe, is success. Success—doing your *best* and being your best at all times.

"For every situation you'll ever face, there will always be a *best* response. For every project, there will be a *best* plan. For every need, there will be a *best* solution. Training you to always have a best response, plan, or solution—training you to be your best in every situation—is a major goal of our program. It typically results in top four percent performance... or better!"

Tapping the page of definitions, Brad smiled and said, "Put this list of definitions behind your Day 7 tab.

"Your assignment yesterday was to list at least ten strong, closed-ended questions and ten strong, open-ended questions. You did that! Starting tomorrow, Day 8, and going through Day 13, we'll develop, expand, and polish some additional questions—questions that will lead you to answers that will guide you into that top four percent."

Joe's eyes widened with excitement. Someone was finally showing him a map he could follow.

"Now, let's talk about your assignments for tomorrow. Your first assignment is continuing to review and polish your open-ended questions and your closed-ended questions. Keep your work behind the tab for Day 6.

"Your second assignment—continue to review and polish your objections and lambs. Keep that work behind the tab for Day 12.

"These first two assignments shouldn't take more than fifteen minutes to a half-hour. Your third assignment is to start developing a list of two hundred new prospective clients for your products and services. For you to join the top four percent, you'll need some new customers. Put this list behind your Day 15 tab. We'll get there next week.

"Joe, we're just a few days away from needing these things, so I'm counting on you to be ready. Don't wait… start today! Some of these lists may seem basic or ordinary, but trust me, they'll make you *extraordinary*."

Testing to see if Joe was *being trained*, Brad asked, "Are you with me, Joe?"

Joe's eyes sparkled as he said, "You're assuming you explained everything perfectly and that I understood. Kind of a bad question, don't you think?"

Brad smiled and nodded, pleased that Joe recognized his trick question. "Good catch, Joe. How about this question? To make sure I clearly explained your assignment, would you summarize what you're going to do before tomorrow's meeting?"

Joe smiled. "Much better, Brad!" Looking down at his notes, he said, "My assignment is to review and polish my open-ended and closed-ended questions. Then review and polish my objections and lambs. And finally, start developing a list of two hundred new prospective customers for my products and services."

Brad closed Joe's binder, nudged it across the table, and scooted out of the booth. "Fantastic! As you complete your assignments, your playbook will become a valuable growing repository of what we call: Third-Brother intelligence. As you polish and practice using your playbook, you'll *reach—and stay—*in the top four percent. I'm looking forward to seeing you again tomorrow."

Day 8: Making the First Call on a New Contact

Joe arrived at the twenty-four-hour diner a few minutes before their normal 5:30 a.m. meeting time, but Brad was already seated in their usual booth. Two cups of coffee were waiting.

Brad smiled. "Good morning, Joe."

"Good morning." Joe sat and placed his Third-Brother Playbook on the table. "And thanks for the coffee."

"You're welcome. How'd it go with your assignments?"

Smiling back, Joe answered, "Really good! But first, I want to thank you. We only met a week ago, and I'm already making significant improvements in my job. I'm using your tools and techniques every day—and they *work*."

"That's great, Joe. Tell me more." Brad stirred his coffee.

"The most significant things you've taught me are surprisingly simple. My goals are now well-defined, and I've never felt so motivated. Each evening, I plan my next day based on those goals. I'm asking better questions, and it's forcing me to be a better listener. And now, after doing yesterday's assignments, I can see the light on the horizon."

Looking out the diner window toward the dark eastern sky, Brad smiled. "It's still dark out there. That light you're seeing isn't on the horizon; it's in your eyes. I can tell you're excited."

"I *am* excited, Brad. I can't wait to dig into the rest of our training days. About the assignments… there were three." Joe ticked them off on his fingers. "First, you told me to review and polish my open-ended and closed-ended questions. Second, polish my objections and lambs. And third, I was to develop a list of two hundred new prospects."

"Very good, Joe. Nice summation."

Joe felt pleased with himself. "Let's start with my third assignment—developing a list of two hundred prospects. Within minutes of searching the Internet, I uncovered thousands of potential prospects. It's amazing how much information is available with just a few mouse clicks. I realized my challenge wasn't *identifying* two hundred new prospects; I needed to reduce the number to two hundred *good* prospects.

"Tell me, Brad, is there a best way to build the list so I'm focused on the best prospects? And I meant to ask yesterday, why two hundred? Why not three hundred or five hundred?"

"Excellent questions, Joe. Let's take them one at a time. The best way to build your list of *good* prospects is to start with research on your existing clients. Let's look at an example of how a little research helped one company dramatically increase its sales in a surprisingly short time.

"Back in the mid-1960s, Xerox dominated the copier market in America. They reached a point where they manufactured more copiers than their people could sell. Everyone in every business was a prospect, but they needed *better* prospects!

"It may be true or an urban legend, but as I understand it, what Xerox did next caused sales to double almost overnight."

Excited, Joe interrupted, "How's that even possible? What did they do?"

"Company leaders made a list of existing customers and looked for similarities," Brad explained. "Basically, they profiled their current customers to see what they had in common.

"Let me ask you a question, Joe; what kind of business would you guess made up the largest percentage of their customers?"

Joe shook his head and said, "I'd guess manufacturing... or maybe the government?"

"Good guesses, Joe—but wrong. Their largest group of customers at the time were lawyers and legal offices. So, Xerox leaders directed their sales force to go through the Yellow Pages—that's like the Google of the olden days—and look up all the lawyers and legal offices in their territories, delete their existing clients, and everyone remaining instantly became an excellent prospect. Their sales skyrocketed!"

Joe shook his head in amazement and asked, "What did they do when they ran out of legal offices?"

Brad continued, "When they needed more prospects, they went to their second largest concentration of clients—the medical profession—and the rest is history!"

"Wow!" Joe said. "The light on the horizon just got a little brighter!" Then he added, "How about my other question—why two hundred? Why not three hundred or five hundred?"

Brad, in a serious tone, said, "That's one of the surprises we found when building our seventeen-day program. *None* of our top four percent salespeople needed more than two hundred good leads to start. Typically, by the time they approached one hundred and fifty of their original two hundred, they were generating so many referrals and new leads, they could theoretically continue… forever."

Joe reflected on the simplicity of Brad's answer. Then, he opened his playbook and flipped the tabs over to reveal a number of pages of neatly typed business names behind the last tab. He turned his binder toward Brad and he said, "These are all the companies in my territory that might use the products and services we provide. There are over eight hundred! I got some from the local Chamber of Commerce and the rest from online research."

Grinning at Joe, Brad said, "Guess what the first part of today's assignment is going to be?"

Joe smiled as he shook his head, gazing at the long list of prospects. "Don't tell me! You want me to profile my current accounts and reduce this list to the two hundred *best* prospects."

"Bingo!" Brad gave two thumbs up. "It might take a few days, but work on it. You'll have it done sooner than you think. Now move them behind the tab for Day 15. That's when we will need them."

Brad turned back to Day 12, where Joe stored his list of potential objections and lambs. Then, looking at Joe's work, he said, "Outstanding! Your lists are coming along nicely. Keep polishing them. They're going to be a critical part of your playbook."

Then turning to Day 6, Brad quickly scanned Joe's closed-ended and open-ended questions. "I see you've added a few new questions. Nice! From now on, whenever you discover a new or better question, be sure to save it here."

Brad closed the binder and slid it back to Joe. "People buy from people they like and trust… Like is important. Trust is essential. If you ask good questions, you have one of the keys to building the 'like' and 'trust' simultaneously. Plus, questions are the tools you use to learn your prospect's real needs. The more you learn, the more you give prospects confidence that you understand their needs and can truly help. The result is them having increased trust in you later when you match your products and services to their needs. Be sure to keep your growing list of questions behind your Day 6 tab."

Joe nodded. "Will do."

Brad handed him another card that read:

Third-Brother Action Step #19

Help your prospects clarify and fill their needs!

It's <u>not</u> about <u>selling</u> products or services.
It <u>is</u> about serving <u>needs</u>!

"Now I see why you've been hammering me with all these question-building assignments," Joe said. "And by the way, when I started to build my prospect list, I found a new business located two miles from here. I called, and just by asking questions, I found the right person to speak to, discovered a possible need, and got an appointment—all in less than five minutes. I have an appointment with one of their key people next week."

"That's excellent, Joe. Before we get into planning that call—and all your future calls—let's summarize one last time the importance of questions as you reach for the top four percent.

"Not to get all religious on you, Joe, but the Bible says if you want to be the master of all, you should be the servant of all. Asking questions is the best way to learn what's important to your prospects. Once we know that, we're better able to serve their known needs. We're also better able to anticipate, and possibly suggest, additional needs they may not even know about. That's exactly what the third brother did!"

Brad signaled for the server to refill their cups. "Now, about that new appointment. What's your plan for that call next week?"

Caught a little off-guard, Joe replied, "Come again?"

"What do you plan to accomplish in your upcoming sales call, and how do you plan to do it?"

Still off-guard, Joe started stumbling through his plan, obviously winging it.

Brad interrupted. "No written plan… right?"

Joe's smile faded as he confessed, "No, not yet."

Brad shook his head. "Joe, if a call is worth doing, it's worth creating an agenda. If it's not worth five minutes to make an agenda with a clear objective and a few good questions, it's probably not worth making the call.

"My guess is 96 percent of all sales calls today are ad-libbed or unplanned. We know there are a million ways to make a first call, but how many *ways* can there be to make a *best* first call? How many *best* ways can there be to make any call?"

Without hesitating or waiting for Joe, Brad answered his own question. "One! There's only one best way. It's not too early to plan that call. And here's some good news: Once you plan a *best* first call, you'll have a template for all subsequent first calls. You can polish and refine the plan, and you may ask different questions, but the basic plan—your basic call agenda—will remain constant.

"You can't build your best rapport and relationships by being less than your best. And no matter how awesome you are without a plan; you'll always be more awesome with one.

"Rapport is defined in one dictionary as 'a close and harmonious relationship in which people understand and effectively communicate with each other.' Unfortunately, Joe, many people confuse rapport with being friends or buddies. You need to remember, most executives do not need another buddy, and if they did, they would meet them outside of work. People who make important decisions are looking for trusted advisors. They want expert problem-solvers—not buddies. Let me give you an example. Remember the three brothers?"

Joe nodded affirmatively. "I do."

"Okay, humor me for a minute. Suppose you were in a jungle, and you found yourself being chased by a lion. Suddenly, you see those three brothers standing at the beginning of three different paths. Each has a sign that says, 'Come this way; I can help you.' Tell me, which of the three would you trust?"

Joe quickly responded, "Obviously, the third brother."

Brad raised his eyebrows. "Obviously?"

Leaning back, Joe said, "Absolutely! All three had the same assignment. The first brother doesn't follow directions, so I wouldn't trust him. The second brother doesn't do any more than he has to, so I wouldn't rely on him either. But the third brother takes action to fix things. He even goes further, proactively taking advantage of opportunities that he identifies. I would, without question, trust the third brother."

"You have chosen wisely Joe! The lion in the story represents problems and opportunities that must be addressed quickly. Even if the first brother were your best buddy, you would still pick the third brother."

Joe's eyes widened. "I see your point!"

"According to data from the U.S. Bureau of Labor Statistics, about twenty percent of US small businesses fail in their first year. By the end of their fifth year, roughly fifty percent have closed their doors. After ten years, only a third of businesses have survived. Every business is chased by lions, but only those with *third brothers* working for them—or calling on them—typically succeed."

Brad paused a moment to let those statistics sink in. Then, he asked, "How might the three-brothers' story impact planning for your upcoming meeting?"

Joe paused to think, then answered slowly, "I need to decide which man—which brother—I'm going to be… *before* the lion approaches."

Brad nodded. "You only get one opportunity to make a good first impression. It's a cliché, Joe, but it's true."

"I'm with you, Brad, but how do I make that call like the third brother would?"

"Excellent question, and your timing is perfect."

Brad pulled out a card and placed it on the table in front of Joe. The card read:

Third-Brother Action Step #20

The "3-B's" of Sales Professionalism

Be Brief - Have an agenda
Be Bright - Ask questions
Be Gone - Leave before they wish you did

"We call these the 3-Bs of sales professionalism. Consider this as a critical guide for every sales call you make as you grow into the top four percent. First, be brief. Have an agenda—a plan—for every call. Whether on the phone or in person, if you aren't prepared, the lion will eat you. Second, be bright. Know what you're going to say—know what you're going to ask. Have several questions prepared so you can listen and learn—so you can encourage your prospect to talk. This means showing up with a prioritized list of both closed-ended and open-ended questions. Third, be gone. Keep the call short and leave before they wish you did!

"After years of tinkering, we found there's one best plan for a first sales call. It's remarkably brief; it helps the salesperson be bright; and it saves time by quickly getting to the meat of the call.

"We don't advocate *canned* sales calls, Joe—we advocate *planned* sales calls. Your first call on a new prospect should sound something like this: 'Thanks for meeting today. I appreciate your willingness to get together. In the next few minutes, I'd like to accomplish three goals. First, tell you a little about us; second, learn more about your company; and third, see if working together makes sense. Does that sound okay?'

"I've never had a prospect answer no to that question, so I typically follow their yes response with this: 'Before I start, are you familiar with our company?'

"If they answer yes, I probe to see what their experience has been. If they answer no, as they usually do, I immediately give my twenty-second overview of the products and services we offer. I end the overview by saying: 'Before going into too much detail about our company and our products, let's go to our second goal. Tell me more about your company and how you currently source the products and services my company provides.'

"From this point on, use your prioritized list of open-ended and closed-ended questions to guide the conversation. Your prospect should now be doing most of the talking. Be sure to stay conversational, asking questions until you're ready to close.

"That's the basic outline we use for a *best* first call."

"That seems simple enough for a first call," Joe said, "but what about follow-up or repeat calls?"

Brad smiled. "You're getting good at this question thing! I mentioned this earlier. One of the best things we found was that subsequent calls follow the same outline—the same process—they follow the same 3-Bs.

"Follow-up and subsequent calls on existing accounts sound similar to first calls, with a few minor exceptions. Second calls and beyond might sound something like this: 'Thanks for meeting again. I appreciate working with you. Today, I would like to cover three *(four... five...)* things during our time together.'

"After listing the items on your agenda, ask if they have goals or ideas they would like to add. After agreeing on the agenda, continue with your meeting.

"Ask questions to identify and clarify new needs. We'll spend more time tomorrow identifying new needs. People make the decision about whether to trust you when they first hear your voice or see your face. So it's essential to start strong. What better way than by being the third brother—using the 3-Bs?"

"That's so simple, Brad. It's genius. You're saying, before each sales call, whether it's a new or repeat call, I need to plan the questions I'm going to ask. Then during each sales call, I need to be brief, bright, and gone—not overstaying my welcome—and never wasting time by winging it or being underprepared. Then, after each call, you're saying I should always do more than I'm asked, expected, or told to do. Finally, all sales calls after the first contact follow the same pattern as the first call. That's what you're saying. Right?"

Brad nodded and smiled. "I'm impressed, Joe! Either you're a great student or I'm a great teacher." Then, laughing, he said, "I think it's a little of both. You know, the Bible says in Proverbs, Chapter 27, 'Iron sharpens iron, and one man sharpens another.' I know you're growing sharper, but did you know your questions and comments are making me sharper, too?"

"Really? Thanks, Brad! That really makes me feel good."

"You're welcome, Joe. Now, let's get back to your upcoming meeting. You need to be prepared like the third brother.

"Imagine that charging lion. Assume you have less than twenty seconds to respond. Can you, in those twenty seconds, describe what you sell and what makes you different from others in your industry?"

Joe wrinkled his brow, searching for a good answer.

Brad continued. "That's the overview I mentioned a few minutes ago. Some people call this their Unique Selling Proposition or USP; others call it an elevator pitch. Whatever you call it, be sure it's short and powerful."

Joe paused, then asked, "Can you give me an example of a good USP?"

"No!" Brad was quick to answer. "That's part of your assignment for tomorrow."

Joe looked shocked by Brad's abruptness, but before he could respond, Brad said, "That's your first assignment for tomorrow. In your own words, I want you to write out *your* Unique Selling Proposition—your elevator pitch—your USP. It's a clear description of not only what you sell but also why people need your product and why they should buy it from you. Read it out loud a couple of times to make sure it sounds good and make sure it takes twenty seconds or less to deliver.

"Your second assignment is to make a bulleted list of the top five to seven products and services you offer. Add one to three benefits for each—benefits that your clients will receive if they buy from you. When we meet tomorrow, I'll explain why you'll need this.

"For your third assignment, go back to the questions you developed on Day 6. Review those questions and continue to polish them."

Brad drained his coffee mug and scooted out of the booth. "I don't think today was our briefest day, but it might be our brightest. I'll see you tomorrow."

Joe shook his head, and both men laughed. "I'll see you in the morning, Brad. Thanks for the iron-sharpening."

"You're welcome. And thanks again for sharpening me." Brad picked up the check again and walked to the cash register.

Day 9: Identifying Needs

5:30 a.m.

Brad walked into the diner early as usual and noticed Joe already seated, waiting with two cups of steaming coffee.

"Good morning, *third brother*," Brad said as he sat down.

"Morning," Joe said, looking up from the two folders he'd prepared, and smiling because of Brad's third-brother compliment.

"Looks like you're ready to be brief, but shouldn't all your work be inside your binder? Why are you still using folders?"

"I want to put everything into my binder. But first, I want to make sure I'm creating and updating my playbook correctly."

Brad nodded. "Understood."

"Thanks, Brad. I appreciate your willingness to meet this early each morning. I have three goals for our time together. First, to review my assignments. Then go through my playbook to make sure I'm developing it correctly. And lastly, cover today's lesson on product knowledge. Is there anything you'd like to add?"

Brad smiled broadly. "That was awesome! A clear plan and a positive start. You'll do great if you begin every meeting this way!"

Joe's face lit up at Brad's praise. "Okay, let's begin. My first assignment was to write an elevator pitch. You called that my Unique Selling Proposition—my USP." Brad leaned in as Joe continued speaking. "I wondered how many words could fill twenty seconds. So, I set a timer for one minute and read an internet news article out loud until the timer went off.

I did this several times, counting the words each time, and discovered I speak at about one hundred and sixty words per minute.

"So, if my speech speed is one hundred sixty words a minute, then twenty seconds is roughly fifty words. I wrote out the typical sentences I use when I'm describing my company and the work I do, and I was shocked! It was over three hundred words. Getting it down to fifty was no easy task."

Joe opened his first folder and handed the contents to Brad.

Brad was surprised. "Joe, this looks like a lot more than fifty words."

"Actually, those are all my notes. You can see it was tough making a short story out of my novel. It was even tougher rewriting my short story in a few sentences."

Brad flipped to the last page and read the final draft of Joe's USP. "Joe, this isn't good—it's great! Some people spend their whole careers without being able to concisely convey what they sell. But you have a twenty-second elevator pitch that communicates your product, service, and unique benefits with clarity."

Joe interrupted. "I'm curious—what do you mean by 'elevator pitch'?"

"OK, Joe, imagine you're going up in an elevator to the tenth floor, and someone gets in on the fifth floor and hits the ninth-floor button. You recognize him as a classmate from college, and in the next few seconds, your friend asks, 'What are you doing now?' You have about twenty seconds to explain it, and if you do it well—if it's effective and memorable like a Super Bowl commercial—your classmate might become a prospect, or remember it well enough—and long enough—to possibly refer you to someone else.

"Yesterday, I used USP or Unique Selling Proposition to mean the same thing as an elevator pitch. Whatever you call it, it needs to clearly describe what you sell and the unique value it brings to your prospects.

"Now your second assignment was to list the top five to seven things you sell. I'm assuming that's in the other folder?"

"Yes!" Joe opened the second folder to reveal another pile of marked-up papers. The top sheet was titled 'Things I Sell.'

"I know you only asked for five to seven, but I came up with twelve, and they're all important. I then added at least three benefits for each product and service. Next, I researched the highest-margin items sold by our company, and guess what? Only two of my top twelve products and services were on the list. That was a shocker! I typically sell only two of our company's highest-margin items. I definitely have room to grow."

"We all do!" Brad confirmed. "The highest-margin products your company sells are probably also the products that bring the most value to your prospects. Knowing the two high-margin things you've sold in the past gives insight into where you've historically focused. Knowing your company's most profitable products and services gives insight into where you can grow in the future."

Brad opened Joe's playbook to Day 8. "Put your first assignment—your elevator pitch—behind this tab. Your second assignment—the top things you sell along with your other research—belongs behind today's tab, Day 9."

Joe quickly inserted his final drafts behind the correct tabs in his binder.

Then flipping back to Joe's tab for Day 6, Brad said, "Let's have a look at your third assignment."

As he browsed through Joe's questions, he said, "This is excellent. Whenever you use these questions in the future, look for ways to polish them even more. You're missing a few important questions, but overall, your lists are quite good."

"I'm missing some?" Joe looked surprised.

"A few. Your current lists of questions will help you identify your prospect's interests and clarify their obvious needs. But if you want your questions to be great, you need to make sure you've included questions in four specific categories. We call them the Four Ds."

Brad pulled four cards out of his inner pocket. "The first D can save tons of time and heartache. It's where you identify the decision process and the influencers."

Brad recited the message from memory as he handed the card to Joe.

"This first D is a great question category for identifying all the people

> # Third-Brother Action Step #21
> *Learn your prospect's decision-making process*
>
> # Decisions
>
> ***Example Questions:*** *When you make decisions on projects like this, do you normally make them on your own, or do you consult with others? Or...When you make decisions like this, what is your decision-making process?*

who are going to *influence* the final decision. Once you know who they are, you can plan meetings to get in touch with as many of those influencers as possible. Acknowledging them gives them comfort that you understand their needs. This will go a long way toward giving the *final* decision-maker the comfort to work with you."

Handing the second card to Joe, Brad continued, "The second question category deals with timing. You need to know the dates that are important to your prospect."

Brad once again quoted the card from memory as Joe read along.

> # Third-Brother Action Step #22
> *Learn your prospect's time constraints*
>
> # Dates
>
> ***Example Questions:*** *What is your timeline for this project? Or... How soon would you like to get started? Or... How soon do you need delivery?*

DAY 9: IDENTIFYING NEEDS

"The third D addresses an elephant that's always in the room," Brad said.

Third-Brother Action Step #23
Learn your prospect's budget considerations

Dollars

Example Questions: *Have you established a budget? Or... Do you have a price range in mind?*

"The fourth D relates to deliverables. Here is where you learn your prospect's expectations. It's important to know early on exactly what your prospect expects you to deliver."

This time, Joe read the card out loud:

Third-Brother Action Step #24
Learn your prospect's delivery expectations

Deliverables

Example Questions: *What must happen between now and when everything is finished for you to say "I couldn't be happier"? Or... Is there anything else you want to see in the end product?*

"Joe, this last D helps you understand your prospect's expectations. You should always strive to exceed them or, if they're unrealistic, address them before proceeding."

"I understand." Joe nodded. "Exceeding expectations makes sense. It's a third-brother thing to do. Do you have any words of wisdom on how I can make sure I truly understand my prospect's expectations?"

"Excellent open-ended question, Joe! First, you need to understand that your prospect's expectations and needs are going to be different from yours. Many Webster salespeople sell what *they* like and really don't care as much about what the prospect likes or wants. So, make sure you understand your prospect's *real* needs."

Joe interrupted, "*Real* needs… are you saying there are *unreal* needs?"

"Let me explain," Brad said. "There are *perceived* needs and there are *real* needs. A perceived need might be for a hand drill. But the real need is to put holes in something. The prospect's perceived need may lead to the best solution, or there may be better solutions. We consider the best solution to always be the one that brings the greatest value to the prospect by filling real needs. That's why we emphasize questions as much as we do. It's critical for the salesperson to point their prospect in the direction of the best solution—the solution that will deliver the greatest value to the prospect.

"Second, make sure your prospect understands their real needs. Webster salespeople only look for needs that add to the sales price or to their profit. The top four percent salespeople look for perceived *and* real needs that bring real value for the prospect. Webster salespeople work to build maximum profit. Third-brother salespeople work to build the maximum functionality, quality, and service. Guess who typically wins?"

"I'm assuming it's not Mr. Webster," Joe smiled

"You have assumed wisely, my young friend. These 'four Ds' are categories of questions that should be addressed early in the sales process. In fact, it's best if you can address them early during your first call.

"Joe, a couple of minutes ago, you asked if I had any words of wisdom on how you can be sure you truly understand your prospect's expectations. My answer—become a great listener! Make sure you understand their perceived *and* real needs!

"Now a question for you, Joe: If being a great listener is important, what's the best way—the best tool—to get yourself into the listening mode—one that will force you to listen?"

Without hesitation, Joe responded, "Ask more questions!"

Brad nodded. "Excellent! That brings us to your first assignment for tomorrow. Review your two current lists of questions—open-ended and closed-ended—making sure you've included questions that cover all four Ds. If necessary, add more questions. As you know, there are many ways to ask these questions, so write them to fit your natural style. Keep all your questions behind your Day 6 tab."

Joe appeared confused, so Brad asked, "How do you feel about all these questions so far?"

"I'm feeling overwhelmed," Joe confessed. "I don't think I can remember them all when I'm with prospective clients."

"That's one of the best parts about our Third-Brother Playbook—you don't have to memorize any of it. You can take your playbook with you to each appointment and refer to Tab 6 any time, before or even during the appointment.

"Selling is an open-book test, Joe, so you should always take your playbook with you; then you can refer to it if you ever go into mental vapor lock—when you want to say something, but your brain seems to disconnect. Keep in mind, it's always better to *have* notes and lists of questions and not *need* them than to *need* them and not *have* them."

Brad continued. "There are two more assignments for tomorrow, but first, I want to share a quick story. About twenty years ago, I read a sales book that put a lot of cookies on the lower shelf. The book's title is *Natural Selling Concepts*.[1] Its principles are basic common sense.

---

1 Carl Bromer, *Natural Selling Concepts, The Best Way to Sell* (937 291-2100) Dayton, OH: B-Elite Publishing, 2005).

"The book includes a story about doctors and how they use their product knowledge to identify needs and make sales. Yes, Joe, doctors are, in fact, salespeople just like you and me. Doctors must quickly and accurately identify needs, and sometimes patients may not even know they have a need. Patients might be aware of a problem, like when a cut is bleeding, or when they have back pain. Or they might be totally unaware of an existing problem, like when a shadow suddenly shows up on a routine x-ray.

"Selling is the same. Sometimes prospects know what they want, sometimes they don't, and sometimes they sense a need but aren't sure why or how to fill it.

"Let me personalize the story for you as best I remember it. Imagine you are out of town, and you wake up with a painful shoulder. You find a local clinic and walk in, holding your shoulder. A nurse approaches, asking, 'What seems to be the problem?' You state the obvious: 'It's my shoulder... I'm in terrible pain.' She writes, 'Sore shoulder' on her clipboard and then leads you to a small white exam room. Eventually, a doctor walks in carrying the clipboard. You read his name tag: Dr. Webster."

Joe laughed, remembering Brad's earlier reference to Webster selling.

Brad continued. "Without looking at the clipboard, Doctor Webster says, 'Before we get started, let me tell you about our medical practice. We've been here for over thirty years. We have seven doctors with more than two hundred years of combined medical experience. Each doctor specializes in a different area. My specialty is hemorrhoids. Last year, I performed over ninety successful hemorrhoidectomies. You may not currently have problems in that area, but there's a chance you will at some point, so let me give you a brief overview of my capabilities. Also, here's some literature showing problems you can develop if hemorrhoids aren't treated properly. Perhaps we might even do a quick examination to make sure everything's okay. Do you have any questions?'

"At that point, you'll probably say, 'I only have one question... Is there another doctor available?'"

Joe and Brad both laughed, and a few heads turned toward them. Brad leaned in and lowered his voice. "Joe, as silly as this scenario sounds, that's how most salespeople sell. They think selling is telling a prospect about their products and services, then handing out literature."

Brad took a deep breath and relaxed in the booth. "Let's look at a better approach. Your shoulder is still in massive pain as Dr. Webster leaves and Dr. Goodquestion comes in. This new doctor now has the clipboard. He sits down and asks, 'What seems to be the problem?' You respond, 'My right shoulder *really* hurts!'

"The doc continues. 'Sharp or dull pain?' You reply, 'Sharp.' Then he asks, 'What were you doing when it happened?' You respond, 'Carrying my suitcase.'

"Then the doc asks, 'Have you seen another doctor about this?' Holding your sore shoulder, you say, 'I don't think so,' even though Dr. Webster is still fresh in your mind.

"'Have we taken an x-ray?'

"'No,' you say.

"'Let's get one and then we'll know how best to proceed.'

"You respond with, 'Sounds good!'

"Dr. Goodquestion just made a sale, and you, without hesitation, willingly bought!

"Take note, Joe, Dr. Goodquestion closed his first sale for an x-ray while getting set up for the second possible sale—surgery. Now the critical question, Joe … What's the difference between Dr. Webster and Dr. Goodquestion?"

Joe thought for a moment, then answered, "Obviously, Dr. Webster talked, but Dr. Goodquestion asked good questions—then he listened."

"Excellent third-brother response, Joe. Telling *ain't* selling; asking is!

"Dr. Webster's credibility and your confidence in him were both undermined by his *telling*. By comparison, Dr. Goodquestion established credibility and built your confidence in him by asking good questions and listening.

"In summary, Joe, Dr. Webster, and Webster salespeople use product knowledge to pontificate, agitate, and regurgitate what they know, primarily with their own interests in mind.

"However, Dr. Goodquestion—and good salespeople—use product knowledge to understand the prospect's *real* need so they can *make* and *explain* their diagnosis. Next, they use product knowledge to *defend* the diagnosis if the patient or prospect asks a question or hesitates. Then they use product knowledge to fill the real need—to *deliver* the best solution.

"Your job, Joe, as it relates to product knowledge, is the same as Dr. Goodquestion's. He used his product knowledge to build good questions while Dr. Webster used his product knowledge to build himself."

Joe raised his hand. "Brad, I'm guilty as charged. That's how I used to sell. I *was* Dr. Webster, and I see it now. It's not surprising I did poorly."

"Well, you're not that guy anymore, Joe. Asking good questions is key to the top four percent, and you're well on your way."

Brad paused. "The last thing we need to cover today are your assignments for tomorrow. We already talked about the first assignment—continue polishing your questions behind your Day 6 tab, and make sure you have questions for each of the *four D's*.

"Your second assignment for tomorrow builds on yesterday's assignment to make a prioritized, bulleted list of the top five to seven products and services you offer. You told me earlier that you came up with twelve. Did you complete the assignment by adding one to three benefits for each of your twelve products and services?"

Joe handed a couple of additional sheets of paper to Brad and said, "I thought this would take longer, but it only took about thirty minutes."

Brad nodded, obviously pleased. Joe had listed three to five possible benefits for each of the twelve products and services. "Excellent job! I asked for one to three benefits for each product and service. You *third-brothered* the assignment! You listed three to five for each.

Put these sheets behind the Day 9 tab. Your second assignment is to go back to the Day 6 tab and make sure you have questions pointing to each of these benefits.

"For example, if your product or service saves time, you might want to add the following questions to your closed-ended list: How much time are you currently taking? What does that cost your bottom line? Ideally, Joe, you will have two or three questions pointing to each of your benefits—for each of your major products and services.

"Your third assignment is to make at least seven cold calls and secure at least one new appointment. Use Dr. Goodquestion's technique, not Dr. Webster's.

Brad looked at the time on his cell phone. "Now I need to be on my way. You ran a tight meeting with a great agenda and good stuff today, Joe. I'll see you in the morning."

Day 10: Qualifying— Finding the Real Needs

5:30 a.m.

Brad walked into the diner early as usual, but for the second day in a row, Joe had arrived even earlier. His young protégé appeared to be focused on reading or writing something.

Pausing near the entrance, Brad remembered himself as a young salesperson trying to find his way. The thought made him smile. Approaching the booth, he said, "Good morning, Joe. You're up early again. How did your cold calls go yesterday?"

Joe looked up as Brad scooted into the booth. "Good to see you too, Brad. The assignment went great. Before I even started, I felt more confident making cold calls than I can ever remember. I had several open-ended and closed-ended questions ready to get the ball rolling. I made twenty calls, spoke with five prospects, and landed two new appointments."

Brad's smile got even wider. "Great! Tell me more about what you learned."

"The first thing was not to waste time doing a lot of research prior to cold calls. You see, before starting my calls yesterday, I spent fifteen minutes researching the *first* call. Then, when I called, all I got was voice mail. After two more calls and two more voice mails, it hit me! I only needed to research if the calls were answered 'live,' and I could do that by asking questions *after* the calls were answered.

"My research time went from about fifteen minutes to less than two minutes per call. Then when I called, if anyone answered, I introduced myself and asked who the best person for me to contact might be. Once I got to the best person, I used questions to identify needs that my company could fill. Whenever prospects used words or terms I didn't know, I asked for clarification, which resulted in prospects talking more, forcing me to be a better listener and helping me to learn more about their needs.

"It was amazing how open most people were when I asked questions and listened instead of droning on about myself. I learned more and was transferred to the best person quicker than I had ever experienced before."

In a serious tone, Brad asked, "So, how did that work out for you?"

Joe quickly answered. "It was great! I still got a lot of voice mails, but I went from an average of three usually unproductive calls per hour to ten or more calls per hour, with two to three that were *very* productive.

"Since my main objective was to land an appointment, as soon as a prospect acknowledged a need, I immediately asked, 'Would you be willing to meet so I can show you how we address those kinds of needs?' I followed your 'Three Bs—Be Brief, Be Bright, and Be Gone,' and the results were awesome!

"Like I just said, two of the five calls resulted in appointments. I confirmed the two appointments and sent a follow-up email to each. My calls were briefer than in the past—also more comfortable and successful. Then, with all the time I saved, I was able to do deeper research into the companies that granted appointments."

"That's outstanding, Joe. When you asked them to clarify the terms that you didn't understand, how did you do it without hurting your ego?"

Joe sat taller to explain. "Before I met you, I would have winged it by pretending to know what they were talking about. Yesterday, I just asked them to explain. It's embarrassing to admit, but I used to be like Dr. Webster. Now I listen twice as much and talk a fraction of what I used to. In fact, most of my talking is just asking more questions.

"Your story about the two doctors transformed my techniques. I'm amazed at how much smoother my conversations are now that I'm asking more questions and listening more than talking."

"Joe, you're well on your way to the top four percent."

Smiling, Joe cocked his head to the side. "*Really?*"

"Yes! You learned three critical requirements for effective selling. You learned to stop winging it. The top four percent salespeople *do not wing it*—they prepare. You learned to stop making assumptions. You asked for clarifications. And, equally important, you learned that you *must* listen. Just like Dr. Goodquestion, you did more listening and less talking. Like I said earlier, telling *ain't* selling—asking is!

"How about the other two assignments?"

Joe opened his playbook to Tab 6, revealing several new pages of questions. The heading on each page was "Product and Service Benefits." Turning the book so Brad could read the new questions, he said, "I combined the first two assignments. I polished my existing questions behind the Day 6 tab while adding new questions that point to my service and product benefits.

"You were right, Brad. It only took about thirty minutes to initially develop my list of benefits. But then, it took almost two hours to develop several questions for each benefit—questions that would point prospects to those benefits. I think the exercise took longer because I'm so conditioned to *telling* people about our products and services; I'm not used to asking questions to help prospects see our products and services as solutions for their needs."

"Lesson learned, Joe. You now have a great inventory of questions for planning and executing excellent sales calls. From now on, whenever you hear or think of a new question, be sure to add it to your playbook behind the Day 6 tab. If you hear or think of a better question than a current one, be sure to replace the less effective question. Are you ready for today's lesson?"

"I am!" Joe responded without hesitation.

Brad leaned forward and put his hand on Joe's playbook. "You already know the most critical skill in selling is asking questions. For today's lesson, we'll focus on the most critical question. We call it the Up-Front Contract or UFC."

Brad signaled the server for a coffee warm-up. "I remember when I first started using Up-Front Contracts—my sales doubled… almost overnight!"

Joe's eyebrows lifted in surprise.

"I didn't achieve top four percent status overnight, but it started the most significant growth spurt in my sales career. Over the next six months, that growth elevated me into the top four percent. That's when I started hiring and training others. Over the next thirty years, my company built and polished the playbook, but it all started with the Up-Front Contract."

Joe interrupted. "So the Up-Front Contract is the most critical question?"

"That's what I'm saying, Joe. Let me explain. The Up-Front Contract is a powerful question. In its most basic form, it asks, 'If I do something for you, will you do something in return for me?' 'If I do A, will you do B?' You're asking the person to commit to a certain course of action *before* you actually do a lot of work—*before* you do a lot of research—*before* you write a proposal. The UFC helps you to find out if there's a real need or opportunity.

"For example," Brad said, as the server poured his steaming coffee. "Do you remember answering 'yes' when I asked, 'If I show you how to get into the top four percent, are you willing to do the work?'"

Joe quickly answered. "Don't tell me. That was an Up-Front Contract?"

"It was. And did you feel obligated at that point to do the work?"

Joe thought for a moment, then slowly answered, "You know... I did!"

"Okay, let's tie it together. In sales, anytime you sense the prospect will agree to move forward, you can qualify their readiness with an Up-Front Contract."

At that point, Brad handed Joe another card. "This might help explain it."

Joe read the card out loud.

Third-Brother Action Step #25
Use Up-Front Contracts to Qualify Needs

Example Up-Front Contracts: *If I am correct about your needs, and can fill them, do I have your approval to proceed? Or... If we can fix the problem, will you move forward? Or... if you like our proposal, can we get started right away? Or... If we can show more benefit than cost, would you be willing to reconsider?*

Brad waited a few moments, then continued to explain. "It's always a question, and it always compels the prospect to agree or, if wrong, to clarify their real need.

"Joe, the four examples show how Up-Front Contracts are typically constructed. But these are *only* examples. Whenever you identify a need, UFCs are a fantastic way to qualify the prospect—to make sure the needs are authentic and to make sure the prospect is ready to move forward.

"If your prospects are ready to proceed, you will get a yes. If they're not ready to proceed, you'll get a no or some other answer, often telling you why they're not ready. In either case, you'll be closer to a sale, assuming a sale is possible. Do you know why UFCs are so great?"

Joe answered meekly, like he was guessing, "Because they get us to a decision faster?"

Brad smiled. "Yes, but they do five things better than any other tool in your bag—five things to qualify the prospect's needs—five things that get you closer to the sale. This is, again, assuming a sale is possible. Sometimes, through no fault of your own, a sale is *not* possible.

"First, UFCs confirm the real need. Second, UFCs confirm the real decision-makers. Third, UFCs identify concerns that will surface later as objections if not properly handled. Fourth, UFCs save time by ensuring the prospect is interested, willing, and able to decide. And fifth, UFCs ask for a commitment in the safest and quickest way… *before* the presentation."

"Would you explain that third advantage again?" Joe asked. "You said UFCs identify concerns that will surface *later* as objections. Can you give me an example?"

"Sure. Suppose you initiate a typical Up-Front Contract by asking, 'If I do A for you, will you do B for me?' And the prospect responds, 'It depends on your delivery dates.' If this happens, the prospect just revealed an important concern about delivery that will affect their decision. Not answering their question properly will likely result in a future objection. The prospect is saying, 'If you do A and *also* have a good answer on delivery, then *maybe* I will do B.' In essence, the prospect just added a clause to your UFC, and you *still* don't have a contract. Essentially, your prospect is saying, 'You must do A and address delivery.'

"So, whenever your prospect adds a clause to your Up-Front Contract, immediately restate the UFC with the clause included. 'If I do A for you and can meet your delivery date, will you do B for me?' Then, if the prospect adds a second clause, restate the UFC again with the second clause included and continue to restate with clauses until the prospect says yes to your UFC. When the prospect says yes, you're ready to proceed with your presentation."

Brad picked up Joe's playbook. "This is probably the most significant technique we learned when developing the program. It's remarkably simple. When implemented, it eliminates guesswork and accelerates the decision-making process for your prospect."

Brad paused a moment before handing another card to Joe and then recited it from memory.

Third-Brother Action Step #26

Whenever you get an objection to your Up-Front Contract, restate the UFC, with the objection as a clause to your revised Up-Front contract.

"Up-Front Contracts are like legal contracts," Brad explained. "When you run into objections, you address them by adding clauses. You continue to add clauses as needed until you have an agreement—until your prospect says, 'Yes!'

"In all my years of selling, Joe, the most clauses I've ever seen added to an Up-Front Contract are three. If that happens to you, your response—your new UFC—should sound something like. 'So, if we do A, B, and C, you're saying we can move forward?'

"A word of caution here, though. Webster people sometimes use Up-Front Contracts to manipulate their prospects. We do *not* want to do that. We want to use Up-Front Contracts to help our prospects make good decisions—ones that will bring a real benefit to them first and ultimately to us as well.

"Joe, I can't overemphasize the importance of Up-Front Contracts. They save time and help you to know what you'll need to cover in your presentation, which is the next step in our program. More on that when we meet again on Monday—Day 11. Before I give you tomorrow's assignment, tell me about those two new appointments you got yesterday."

Joe's face lit up as he responded, "I'm glad you asked. I landed two appointments—TRB and Compton-Daniel Manufacturing."

Brad seemed surprised. "Did you say *TRB*?"

Joe answered, "Yeah, TRB… Are you familiar with them?"

Brad nodded. "I am… and I've heard of Compton-Daniel as well. Aren't they both located in Columbus?"

Joe affirmed their location, adding, "Columbus was just added to my sales territory. We recently lost a couple of salespeople, and rather than replace them, all our territories were realigned. I'm excited to have new accounts to call on, especially now that you're helping me."

Brad pulls out his pocket calendar and asks, "When are your appointments?"

Joe grabbed his calendar and, after a quick look, answered, "TRB is this coming Wednesday afternoon at 3:00 pm, and my Compton-Daniel appointment is three weeks out."

"Wow, Joe, the timing is perfect. We have a few more things to cover today. Tomorrow will be a well-deserved day of rest for both of us. Then we'll cover presenting on Monday—that's Day 11 in our program. On Tuesday, we'll hit objections and lambs, and on Wednesday morning, we'll talk about closing. That's perfect timing for your Wednesday afternoon appointment with TRB."

Brad signaled for the server to bring more coffee. "Now for Monday's assignment…"

Joe pulled out a pad of paper. "I'm ready when you are."

"Your first assignment for Monday is to go back one more time and review the objections you started listing on Day 5. Make sure you've included *all* the objections you've ever heard, and I want you to even add objections you think you might hear in the future. It's important to be as complete as possible. Those go behind the Day 12 tab in your playbook."

Joe spun the playbook around to his side of the table and opened it to Day 5. Removing several sheets, he put them behind his Day 12 tab. Then, looking up, he said, "You know, Brad, I've been polishing this list for almost a week, and I'm amazed how few objections there really are."

Brad nodded and smiled. "Keep polishing. Tuesday is Day 12, and that's when we'll complete the section on objections and lambs. Then, like I said a minute ago, on Wednesday morning, we'll cover closing.

"In the meantime, your second assignment is to write a preliminary agenda for the TRB meeting you have scheduled on Wednesday afternoon. Bring the agenda on Monday. We're going to talk about making presentations on Monday, and we can polish your preliminary TRB agenda at that time.

"I think you're going to be surprised, Joe. Presenting isn't like what you see on TV. It's not standing in front of a group of executives, impressing them with your wise speech about *your* solutions to *their* problems while they sit silently admiring your genius. That's not what presenting is like in the real world! In fact, there's a name for that kind of presentation—it's called a 'dog and pony show.'

"In the real world, presenting is the part of the selling process where you use questions to understand your prospect's needs—questions to get your prospect to understand and agree that your products and services will generate a positive ROI. And finally, questions to guide them to make *wise* decisions.

"Listen carefully, Joe—a decision is considered wise if it does two things. First, if it brings more benefit than cost. And second, if it helps the prospect accomplish their goals.

"Use questions to discover your prospect's real goals and needs. Whether it's a company or an individual, you're ready to help your prospect make wise decisions after you do. So, start your agenda for your first meeting with questions to learn your *prospect's* goals and needs. Then complete your agenda by asking yourself: What do you want to accomplish in that meeting, and what questions can you ask to help the prospect see you as a good solution for their needs and goals?

"By the way, Joe, what *do* you want to accomplish in that meeting?"

Somewhat sheepishly, Joe responded, "I'd like to make a sale."

Shaking his head, Brad smiled. "That's a good result, Joe, but just to make sure I'm driving the point home—you must have an agenda or you'll have to wing it! And 'wingers' aren't the best winners! If closing the sale is your goal, you'll have to do more than wing it. You'll need an agenda that gives you and TRB the best path to the sale."

Joe interrupted, "I know—there's only *one best* way, right?"

"Right! And remember, good salespeople don't wing it—they plan. So Monday, I want you to show me a plan that will take you through the process from the opening to the close. I want to see the questions you will use to guide TRB to make *wise* decisions that will benefit their company—and yours as well.

"This is what it's all about—getting results that benefit everyone involved! Are you ready to build an agenda that will deliver results for TRB? An agenda that will also deliver results for your company, your boss, yourself, and for me?"

"Brad, I'm ready! I know I can do this for TRB, for me, and for my company. But help me understand—what's in it for you?"

The older man paused and then grinned. Joe didn't know that Brad knew more about TRB than he was letting on. "Good question, Joe. There might be more in it for me than you know. I'll see you Monday."

Feeling a bit overwhelmed and a little confused about Brad's last answer, Joe sheepishly asked, "Can we possibly meet tomorrow?"

"Joe, tomorrow is Sunday! You need a day of rest, and so do I. You need to be fresh next week. Like we discussed before, I used to work Sundays, but I stopped doing that a long time ago. Tomorrow is already blocked for my family. I committed to take a day of rest each week and to always put my family first. It started years ago when I met an expert on efficiency who suggested I take one day each week to rest. If you're interested, maybe someday I'll introduce him to you."

Day 11: Presenting

5:30 a.m.

Early Monday morning, Joe entered the diner with a spring in his step. The familiar sound of bells hitting the entrance door alerted Brad, who sat reading his Bible, already having his second cup of coffee.

"Good morning, Joe."

Tucking the little Bible and his reading glasses into his pocket, Brad continued, "I'm excited to see how you did with those assignments from Saturday."

Joe quickly sat down, a big smile lighting up his face. "It *is* a good morning."

Brad rested his arms on the table. "You seem pretty confident today."

Joe's smile grew larger as he opened his playbook and pushed it closer to Brad. "Check this out!"

Brad put his reading glasses back on and started leafing through the playbook. He couldn't conceal his pleasure—or his surprise. All of Joe's handwritten pages were now neatly typed and organized. "Joe, this is awesome. First-class third-brother work!"

Brad flipped the tab to Day 12 in Joe's playbook and said, "Let's look at your first assignment. You were to go back one more time and review the objections you started listing on Day 5. This section on objections seems to be getting *smaller*."

Joe interrupted. "Yeah, I thought it would grow as I listed more and more objections, but it didn't. In fact, I think I have fewer objections now than last week!"

"You're learning one of the most important lessons in sales, Joe; you're learning there really are *not* millions of objections—only a few. It just seems like millions because there are millions of ways to say them. You can say, 'Your price is too high,' 'That costs too much,' 'It's too expensive,' 'I don't want to pay that much,' and a million other things about cost. But the bottom line—pun intended—is that all those objections boil down to just one basic objection: 'Why should I pay that much?'

"We'll dive deeper into objections and lambs tomorrow. The work you've done so far is going to pay off in a big way.

"Now, let's have a look at your second assignment. You were to write up a preliminary agenda for the meeting with your new prospect. I think you said the company's name is TRB?"

"That's right, I'll be seeing TRB on Wednesday afternoon."

Brad flipped open the Day 11 tab, and his smile immediately affirmed his approval.

"Super! You created a brief agenda with some excellent 'first-call' questions. I know I'm sounding like a broken record by repeating myself so much, but I have to say it again, this is *excellent* third-brother work!" Then, looking over the single neatly typed page, Brad asked, "Is this the agenda you plan to use when you call on TRB?"

Joe answered, "Yes… and no. It started as an agenda for this week's meeting, but then I thought, 'Why reinvent the wheel for every new presentation?' So, I decided to develop a template that could be used to plan *every* first call. I listed several of my best current clients and asked myself, 'What would be the best questions to ask if I were making a first call on each of them?' I listed questions that would help me learn their needs and some additional questions that would encourage them to see the benefits they would gain by working with my company. Visualizing current clients and how they benefit from our products and services really helped as I developed the template. Now all I have to do is change

DAY 11: PRESENTING

the company name, tailor the questions for each new prospect, and I've got it—a customized, *best* sales meeting agenda."

Brad looked impressed. "You know, Joe, you're growing into a *top-four-percenter* faster than I can teach it."

Joe's grin expanded into a full-blown look of pride. Recognizing the younger man's rapidly inflating ego, Brad smiled, shook his head, and changed the subject.

"Okay, Joe, are you ready for today's lesson?"

"Isn't that what we're talking about? Isn't the agenda the outline for the presentation?"

Brad nodded. "It is. But keep in mind, your presentation is essentially executing your agenda—with questions. Like I said on Saturday, use questions to understand your prospect's needs. Then use questions to get agreement that your products and services will bring a positive ROI. And finally, ask questions that will guide them to make *wise* decisions. Your agenda template does that nicely for calls on new prospects.

"Now, let's talk about the primary focus for all your presentations—all your calls—new calls and repeat calls on existing clients.

Brad pulled out a card and slid it over to Joe. It read:

Third-Brother Action Step #27

Use an agenda with pre-planned questions to fill your part of the UFC (Listen more than you talk!)

Even a fool who keeps silent is considered wise; when he closes his lips, he is deemed intelligent. Proverbs 17:28

A fool takes no pleasure in understanding, but only in expressing his opinion. Proverbs 18:2

Joe looked up and frowned. "What's this, Brad? Are you getting ready to thump me with your Bible?"

Brad laughed and shook his head. "Not yet. Just sharing a couple of principles that were true three thousand years ago and are still true today. You should know by now, 'Telling *ain't* selling… "

Joe finished the sentence… "Asking is!"

Brad nodded, adding, "The bottom 96 percent of salespeople talk too much and listen too little! They make long, boring presentations. The presentation is critical, but it's a small piece of the total process.

"Remember, *the purpose of the presentation is to fill your part of the UFC!* Once you do, it's natural to move to the close. Always ask for the order. Always ask for the commitment.

Joe responded confidently, "If all goes well tomorrow, I'll do that. I have a couple of closing questions ready to go."

"Not to burst your balloon, Joe, but what if all *doesn't* go well? What if you get another objection?"

Without hesitation, Joe opened his playbook to Day 12 and pointed to several pages of objections and neatly typed responses. "I think I'm ready."

Once again, he turned the book around to show Brad several pages of objections and neatly typed responses.

"This is good, Joe. How many objections and lambs do you have?"

"About fifteen objections and one or two lambs for each. I used to have more, but I found some objections listed several times, using different words. The more I polish the list, the more redundancies I discover… and the more the list *shrinks*."

"Not to worry," Brad reassured him. "Tomorrow, I'll show you how your list might get even shorter.

"One other thing, Joe, if you can't close, you should at least set up your next appointment. The best time to do this is when you're still with your prospect."

Joe responded with noticeable confidence. "This is starting to make sense!"

"Good! So, your first assignment for tomorrow is to continue to polish your objections and lambs. Be sure to capture the lambs that have been successful for you in the past.

"Your second assignment is to list questions for closing the sale. Those are questions that ask the prospect to take the next step—that is, to buy. It might seem daunting, but just like objections, there are only a few closing questions, so it's worth the effort to capture them and commit them to memory. Keep your closing questions behind your Day 13 tab."

Brad took a deep breath. "You know, Joe, people are always looking for the magic pill in sales. But this process—this system—isn't magic. It's the *best* step-by-step procedure for consistent year-over-year success. Is it hard? Only at first! But the more you practice, the more it becomes second nature."

"I'm looking forward to it!" Joe said.

Brad gave him a thumbs-up and scooted out of the booth.

Day 12: Handling Objections

5:30 a.m.

Joe walked into the diner promptly at five-thirty. Looking over at their usual booth, his stomach sank. Brad wasn't there! Instead, a fit-looking young man, maybe in his thirties, was sitting in *their* booth.

The young man looked comfortable with his coffee, reading a little black book similar to Brad's. For a split second, Joe closed his eyes and shook his head. It *is* Brad… but it *can't* be. He's too young. Where's Brad? Why is that young guy sitting there? *That's our booth!*

The young man looked at Joe, stood, and started walking toward Joe. As he approached, Joe pretended to look for someone else in the almost empty diner.

Softly smiling, the young man greeted Joe. "Hi, we've never met, but based on that look on your face, I'm sensing something's wrong."

The guy's words seemed eerily familiar, and Joe tried to think where he might have heard them.

"Do you mind if we sit?" the young man said. "I already have a booth."

Joe paused as the stranger walked back to the booth. *This isn't right.* He tapped the young man's shoulder and asked, "Hey, I'm sorry, but do I know you?"

The young man turned and smiled again. "Are you Joe?"

Confusion washed over Joe's face. "I am," and then, without hesitation, he asked, "What's your name?"

"I'm Brad Roberts. Come on, let's sit down. My dad will be here any minute. By the way, coffee is on its way for you and Dad, just the way you both like it." He laughed. "I knew you'd be confused. Everyone says I look just like my dad."

Joe wasn't amused, but he was relieved. He followed Brad's son to the booth. "So, you're Brad's son. What do you do for a living?"

As they sat, young Brad responded, "I'm currently on active duty in the Air Force, but I'm home for a short leave visiting my dad. He's been my hero and mentor all my life. Right now, I'm talking with dad about a major career decision. Dad told me you were going through his seventeen-day program, and he asked if I could meet with the two of you today."

The server delivered two more cups of coffee. Joe looked up and thanked him.

"By the way, when Dad gets here, please call me BJ. It's short for Brad Junior and less confusing when my dad and I are in the same room."

Just then, Joe heard the bells ring over the door—he turned and was relieved to see Brad Senior, who walked over and slid into the booth next to his son. BJ gave his dad a one-armed embrace.

"Joe, I asked BJ to join us this morning because he's been applying today's lesson in his work, and BJ's not even in sales."

"Really?" Joe said as he opened his playbook and looked at BJ. "You're *not* in sales, and yet you have to answer *prospect* objections?"

Brad reached over and pulled Joe's playbook closer. "Not exactly, but kind of. BJ is a fighter pilot. In his line of business, emergencies are often life-or-death situations. When he has an emergency, he doesn't have the luxury of strategizing and sleeping on it. He has to react immediately, or he could die—and that would definitely mess up his whole day… not to mention mine!"

"In sales," Brad continued, "it's similar. When a prospect knocks you off balance with an objection, you don't have time to think and plan. You've got to react immediately, and the quality of your reaction will determine your success. You may not die, but if you're not prepared, it will hurt your meeting, and it could impact your whole career."

"Other than reaction time," Joe asked, "how do jet fighter emergencies tie in with objections in selling?"

BJ leaned in and, with a grin, said, "Mary had a little… "

"Not you too?" Joe said. The three men laughed.

BJ continued, "When you have an emergency in a fighter jet, like if your wing gets shot off, you only have a split second to react. Unless your immediate reaction is an automatic, *best* response—a lamb—you could die."

Joe flashed back to Brad's lesson on Day 5. His expression brightened. "So, you're saying that unless I have an automatic best response when I hear an objection, I'll probably crash?"

Brad answered, "In a manner of speaking, yes. That's what we're talking about, but that's *not* the key."

Joe felt confused. "Okay, but you said memorizing and reviewing is how you program lambs into your brain. Now you're saying that's not enough?"

Brad and BJ replied in unison… "Correct!"

Brad continued. "Head knowledge is important. That's where your mental habits are stored. But physical habits are just as essential when the bullets are *flying* over your head! Having the best response programmed into your brain is the critical first link in the chain. The second link—and the key—is preprogramming your *physical responses* too.

"Look at it this way, Joe. Selling is a contact sport. Knowing the automatic, most appropriate response or lamb is critical, but just as important, is physically saying it out loud. That's why role-playing is so important; it gives you physical practice using lambs. Think of it like simulating a combat mission while bullets are flying all around you."

Brad patted his son on the arm. "You see, BJ flies a $100-million jet for work. It requires a lot of head knowledge and, just as crucial, a lot of physical practice in and outside a simulator. He's proficient now and combat-certified. But before he was ever allowed to fly solo, he had to demonstrate physical execution skills safely on the ground. That required a lot of hours practicing in a flight simulator—kind of like role-playing."

Joe perked up. "I think I see where you're going, but I'm not sure how to get there. Where do I go to get training in a 'selling simulator'?"

Brad chuckled. "That's why I invited my son to join us this morning."

Joe's face lit up as he asked, "So, BJ has a selling simulator?"

Brad smiled and shook his head. "I love your sense of humor, but no, he doesn't own a selling simulator."

BJ also shook his head as he grinned and responded to Joe. "I worked several summers doing sales for my dad during college. Initially, it was tough. It seemed like there were literally millions of variations of objections from prospects."

Looking briefly at Brad and then back to Joe, he asked, "Has my dad asked you to write all the objections you can think of?"

Joe nodded.

"And did you notice the more you worked on your list, the shorter it got?"

Joe pointed to his playbook and said, "My first list had over a hundred. Today, I'm down to eleven."

Brad and BJ exchanged glances as BJ asked, "Joe, you must be getting close to the end of your ground training. Has Dad told you how many there *really* are?"

Joe looked at Brad and raised his eyebrows, but didn't answer. "Joe, I gave you two assignments yesterday. The first was to clean up your list of objections and lambs. You may be down to eleven, but if you continue to polish your list and eliminate redundancy, you'll find there are really only eight. Surprisingly, they're the same for every industry—every product, every service, and every attempt to persuade. If you memorize lambs for each one, you're halfway ready to fly."

Joe pushed back. "Halfway? If there are only eight objections, shouldn't I be closer than halfway?"

BJ jumped in, "Joe, the head knowledge is only half! The other half, like we just said, is skilled execution. Once I memorized all the emergency procedures for my jet, I had to practice in the simulator until I could execute without hesitation—sometimes without even thinking. My response to emergencies, mental and physical, *had* to be *automatic*!"

Joe was silent for a moment and stared out the window before responding. "Okay, I know I can memorize the lambs—but I still have two questions. How do I get down to eight objections? And where do I find a sales simulator?"

Taking a card from his pocket, Brad responded. "First, let's look at the eight." Brad then handed the card to Joe, who read it out loud:

Third-Brother Action Step #28
Build Lambs for the Eight Objections

1. **No need**
2. **No want**
3. **No time** *(no hurry; want to wait; stall)*
4. **No money** *(way too much)*
5. **No money** *(a little too much)*
6. **No trust** *(don't know you)*
7. **No trust** *(do know you)*
8. **Legitimate constraint**

Joe looked up from the card as Brad said, "Let's look at the first two objections—no need and no want. Most of the time, when you hear a 'no need' or 'no want' objection, what your prospect is really saying is, 'I *do have* a need for the product or service—but I don't have a need for *your* product or service!' It's actually a trust objection.

"If you ever hear a real 'no need' or 'no want' objection, your best approach is to start over. Go back to what you learned on Day 9 about identifying needs and use the list of questions you've been building. Ask more questions to identify or uncover needs or wants that aren't being satisfied. Continue until you find a real need—or until you find there *is* no real need to fill. If you *do* find a real need that you *can* satisfy, qualify the need with an Up-Front Contract; if you *can't* find a real need, politely thank your prospect, and end the call.

"The next six objections can come at you like emergencies in a jet fighter. If your responses are good, you have a better chance of walking away from a safe landing. In a jet fighter, these responses are called emergency procedures; in selling, they're called lambs.

"Joe, here's what you need to know. Objections happen. When they do, it's critical to have lambs and execution skills. Even though there are only six more categories of objections, there are millions of variations of those objections. It's impossible to have millions of lambs, so we use a technique BJ learned years ago, flying jet fighters.

BJ broke into the conversation. "It's true, Joe, years ago, when I was home on leave after my first combat tour, dad and I were talking late into the evening. Mom had already gone to bed, so I shared a few war stories with Dad."

"They made my hair curl," Brad said. "He told me about a couple of his in-flight emergency procedures, and then suddenly, the lights came on for both of us. We realized way back then that objections in selling may not be life-and-death emergencies, but the same *principles* applied. That is, if you have an immediate, most appropriate, best response, then you'll come out better on the other side."

Brad looked at BJ and asked, "What *do* you do if your wing gets shot off?"

Without a blink, BJ rattled off his answer. "Tuck your elbows; tuck your knees; raise the handles; trigger squeeze."

BJ quickly added, "It's called our Master Emergency Procedure. The same concept is applicable in sales, Joe. When you hear an objection, your immediate reaction often determines winning or losing the sale. If you snooze, you lose!"

Joe sat speechless, with a trace of a growing smile.

Brad pulled out a new card and placed it on the table. "It's one of the most significant steps that helped our people reach the top four percent. We call it our Master Lamb."

Third-Brother Action Step #29

Internalize the Master Lamb

- **Acknowledge**
- **Probe**
- **UFC**
- **Close**

"The Master Lamb is our emergency procedure for all objections. Memorize it! Practice it! Make it a part of you! Internalize it until it's as familiar as Mary's little lamb—until it's automatic!

"From now on, Joe, if someone were to awaken you from a sound sleep and ask what to do when your prospect objects, you should immediately recite the Master Lamb. You should immediately say, 'Acknowledge—Probe—UFC—Close!'"

"Seems simple enough to memorize the Master Lamb," Joe admitted. "But you said having the best response programmed is only the *first* critical link; the *physical skills* also need to be programmed. So, where *is* this sales simulator? When do I get a chance to drive it?"

Brad smiled while shaking his head. "Not so fast. I know you're all fired up, but there are a few things to consider before taking off. Let's look at the four steps in the Master Lamb.

"First, *acknowledge*—never ignore or sidestep an objection. Confront it head-on. You don't need to agree, but you *do* need to acknowledge it. For example, if your prospect says your price is too high, you can respond, 'I don't blame you for not wanting to spend too much.' If your prospect says let me think it over, you can acknowledge by saying, 'I don't blame you for not wanting to make a hasty decision.' Joe, it's always good to let your prospects know you're listening and understanding their concern.

"The next step is to *probe*—ask questions to better understand your prospect's concerns. If they're stalling, you might say, 'Usually, when clients hesitate to make a decision, it's a sign they still have unanswered questions. What questions do you have that are causing you to hesitate?' Continue to probe until you uncover—or discover—a real need that your product or service can satisfy.

"The third step is to *ask for a new Up-Front Contract*. Then, assuming you're able to fulfill your part of the UFC, the fourth and final step is the *close*."

Joe looked at BJ, then back to Brad, and said, "Now I see why you had me building those lists of questions. They're questions that bring the real needs to the surface."

Brad slid the Master Lamb card over to Joe. "That's right. Those questions are important. Continue polishing them. You'll use them for the rest of your career. And now, I think we're ready to talk about the sales simulator."

Joe's eyes brightened, and he felt a stirring of excitement. "Alright! About time!"

Brad calmly opened his hands and confessed, "No such thing. It hasn't been invented yet—and probably never will be. You see, there are only a few actual objections, and you can practice them anytime with your sales manager or coworkers."

Joe shook his head. "That's too simple!"

"You're right," Brad said. "And that's why so few salespeople do it. Here's what I want you to do. When you get to work today, ask a coworker to help you practice answering objections. They'll probably look at you like you have two heads. They don't know there are only eight total objections—actually, only six if you just count the ones that need the Master Lamb.

"Practice using the Master Lamb. You'll be amazed how quickly you get proficient. Then tomorrow, during your sales call, you'll have another opportunity to practice. The difference? Tomorrow's call with TRB isn't practice; it's real!

"Speaking about tomorrow, Joe, let's look at your closing questions from yesterday's assignment."

Joe took a deep breath and opened his playbook to his list of closing questions.

Brad read quickly through the list. Looking up, he said, "It's short, but that's okay. We still have a little work to do, and we'll cover closing before your meeting tomorrow. Closing is more than getting an order; it's getting someone to take an action that benefits both them and you. Tomorrow's a big day. If you were a pilot, it would be like your first solo flight. After we discuss closing tomorrow, you'll be prepared for a successful mission.

"Today, your assignment is to confirm tomorrow's meeting and get your agenda ready. Then visualize how the meeting will go, including seeing yourself driving there and walking into the building. Finally, see yourself asking questions and addressing objections using lambs."

Joe took another deep breath.

"This is what it's all about," Brad said. "Review your playbook in preparation for tomorrow's meeting with your prospect. Remember why we've met each morning over the last two weeks.

"Tomorrow morning, we'll go over closing, and that will complete the pre-call portion of your playbook. Only those who've been faithful to do *all* the assignments get this far, Joe. Closing is the *easiest* part of the process if you're prepared—the *hardest* part if you're *not!*"

Brad locked eyes with Joe. Slowly and confidently, he said, "You're ready for this. I'm proud of you and counting on you to apply all the tools I've taught you. They're not just *my* tools anymore; they're *your* tools, and I know you'll use them well."

"I'll get right to work."

"Joe, would you mind if BJ and I stay a bit longer? We'd like a few minutes to catch up alone."

That request caught Joe a little off-guard. Brad was always the first to leave; but now he was politely hinting for Joe to leave first.

"Sure. Everything okay?"

Brad's tone became serious. "Actually, Joe, things have been a bit tense lately. I'm working on a major project and was up last night hammering out a few details. That's why I was late this morning. I needed my beauty rest. I apologize for being tardy. Everything's fine now."

Trying to keep things light, Joe suggested, "Well, if it's all good now, maybe you can shadow me on my appointment tomorrow afternoon."

Smiling again, Brad shook his head. "You'll do fine. Just follow the training. I assure you, no matter who shows up, you will impress them. And I know you'll feel proud when you walk out."

"Thanks for your faith in me," Joe said, scooting out of the booth. He shook hands with BJ. "Really nice meeting you; you're lucky to have Brad as your dad."

BJ stayed seated while shaking Joe's hand. Then, with a big smile, said to Joe, "We're *both* lucky. Nice meeting you, too. I'll be praying for a successful mission for you tomorrow."

Joe was caught a little off-guard; he wasn't used to hearing people say they'd pray for him. He thanked BJ again as he turned to leave.

Day 13: Closing—Precipitating Action

5:30 a.m.

Joe arrived at the diner a couple of minutes before five-thirty. Seeing Brad in their usual booth, reading his Bible with his morning coffee, put Joe at ease as he walked over.

"Good morning, Joe."

"Morning, Brad. You look a little tired. Trouble sleeping? You're not worried about my big sales call later today, are you?"

Brad cracked a soft smile as he placed his small Bible in his pocket. "Tired? Yes. Worried? No. Just working long hours on an ownership transition plan. It's a lot of hard work. How about you? Are you ready for today's sales call on TRB?"

Joe took a deep breath, and said, "*You* may not be worried, but *I* am! This is my first big call since we started meeting, and I don't want to mess it up."

"That makes sense. If you weren't a little nervous, I'd think you were taking the call for granted. You put in the hours; you completed each assignment. There's no doubt in my mind. You're ready!"

Brad went on, "Even so, it's good to be a little nervous. Will the call be perfect? I doubt it. But I absolutely believe it will be way better than it would have been thirteen days ago?!"

Joe smiled with a big sigh. "You know Brad, thanks to you, I believe

I am ready."

Brad nodded an acknowledgment of Joe's gratitude.

"Yesterday, Brad, you told me to confirm today's meeting, get my agenda ready, and visualize how the meeting will go, including seeing myself driving there and walking into the building. So, I pictured myself going to TRB, meeting with a few key people, asking questions, addressing objections, using lambs, and closing new business. So, done—done—and *done*!"

"Excellent! Sounds like you're ready."

Joe opened his playbook to Day 13. "But I'm still a bit confused about something."

"What's that?" Brad asked.

"Yesterday, you implied my list of closes was too short and needed work. But now, you're saying I'm ready to make the call."

Brad raised his index finger and interrupted. "Actually, I said, 'Your list is short, and we have a little work to do.' Your list wasn't *too* short. It just wasn't the *best*. How many *best* closes are there, anyway?"

Joe thought for a second. Then, with open hands. "Okay, I know there's only one best of anything. So, are you saying I only need *one* closing question?"

Brad leaned forward. "Do you remember me saying, 'Closing is the hardest thing to do if you're *not* ready… and the easiest if you *are*'?"

Joe nodded.

"And do you remember me saying there are only a few objections, but millions of ways for prospects to say them?"

"I remember. But what's your point?"

"Let me ask you, Joe: What would be better than having *one* closing question that you could easily ask a million different ways?"

Joe's face lit up in anticipation. "You're kidding, right?"

"Nope! I'm telling the truth. There's only one best closing question, and I'll share it in a few minutes. First, let's start with a quick illustration about the importance of closing. There's an old story about a boxer.

Before his fight, he got down on one knee and bowed his head, appearing to be praying. He raised his head, crossed himself, then looked up and pointed his index finger skyward. A guy in the audience asked a priest sitting next to him, 'What does *that* mean?' The priest paused a moment, and answered, 'Actually, it doesn't mean a thing if he can't box.'

"Joe, selling is similar. All the work and preparation up to this point means nothing if you can't—or don't—close."

Brad paused to let that sink in as he slowly removed four cards from his briefcase. Handing the top card to Joe, he said, "First, let's define a new term, 'Domino closing.'"

The card read:

Third-Brother Action Step #30
(Closing 1 of 4)

ABDC—Always Be Domino Closing

★ Domino closes move things forward
★ They precipitate action
★ They encourage the prospect to take the next step
★ They ask for a decision to tip the next domino

"Joe, the bottom 96 percent of salespeople see closing as one final dangerous place where all success and failure resides. However, the top four percent of salespeople see closing as a process. They see closing as a series of smaller steps—each step like nudging the next domino in a continuous chain reaction that eventually leads to filling a real need.

"Remember our definition of selling: Finding people who have needs that our products and services can satisfy and filling those needs in such a way that they—and we—both make a profit or gain.

"Domino closing is something you do throughout the selling process. It might be getting the prospect to agree to meet again for a demonstration. It could also mean getting an appointment to present to a group, such as a board of directors. Whether it's one domino or a string of many, domino closing is *nudging* the next domino in line until you eventually nudge your prospect to make a final decision—a decision to purchase your product or service.

"Let's go back to the beginning. From then until now, closing has always been about asking questions. The first set of questions helps you understand your prospect's needs. Your UFC questions help qualify the needs. And now, your domino closing questions get the prospect to take action toward filling their needs with your products or services. Domino closing questions nudge the process forward."

Joe shook his head in disbelief. "You always make it sound so simple!"

Brad handed the second card to Joe. "It *is* simple! But let's look at the timing. Knowing *when* to close can be a bit tricky."

Joe read the second card out loud:

Third-Brother Action Step #31
(Closing 2 of 4)

Test the Water with Trial Closes

★ Use trial closes to make sure the prospect is ready to say yes

★ Trial closes ask for opinions

Joe looked up from the card. "Can you give me an example of a trial close and a domino close?"

Brad paused and then asked, "Joe, how do you *feel* about all the assignments up to now?"

Joe was confused by the non-answer but replied, "They're a lot of work, but I feel good about them. They've helped me a lot."

Before Joe could continue, Brad interrupted him. "That was a trial close. I asked your opinion, and you told me you were ready for the next domino. It's safe at this point to give you another assignment—to ask you to take the next step. If you had said you were tired of all the assignments, it *wouldn't* have been a good time to go for the next domino.

"Basically, trial closes ask for the prospect's opinion. Their answers let you know if they are ready for the next domino in the closing process.

"It's all about *best* timing. In other words, if I ask if you prefer option one or option two—a trial close—and you respond that you don't like either option, that's probably not a good time to use a domino close. However, if you respond, 'I love option two,' then it's a safe time to use a domino close—like saying, 'Great! If there are no other questions, let's write it up.'"

Brad slid the third card over to Joe, who then it read out loud:

Third-Brother Action Step #32
(Closing 3 of 4)

Earn the Right to Push!

The "Pushy Principle"
Pushing a prospect to make a good decision is good, but you must first earn the right to push!

"The 'Pushy Principle'?" Joe said, chuckling.

Brad nodded with a smile. "That's right. Do you remember the story from a few days ago about the two doctors?"

Joe nodded "I do."

"Dr. Goodquestion earned the right to say, 'You need surgery.' He earned the right by asking questions. He earned credibility by asking questions that demonstrated he understood the patient's needs. Dr. Goodquestion earned the right to tell the patient what to do. He *earned the right* to push."

Joe looked up from the card. "Brad, you're doing it again. You're making it sound *too* simple."

Brad hesitated, appearing to search for a good reply. "That's the beauty of the pushy principle. It *is* simple. Let me give another quick illustration. First, Joe, do you trust me?"

Joe quickly responded, "I wouldn't be here if I didn't."

"Excellent. Pretend you're going to Asia on a mission or business trip, and let's assume a cholera epidemic is raging there. In a casual conversation, I ask if you've had your cholera shots, and you respond that you hate shots and you'll only be there a week. At that point, if I said, 'Joe, don't be reckless; get the shot!' would you be offended, or would you think I care about you?"

"I definitely wouldn't be offended."

"That's because I've earned the right to push. I've earned your trust over the last two weeks by asking you questions and listening to your answers. Telling you not to be reckless is a fairly pushy statement. But you don't recognize it as pushy because you know I care. In other words, *I earned the right to push!*"

"So, Brad, you're saying I need to be a pushy salesperson?"

"What I'm saying, Joe, is you need to *earn the right* to tell your prospects what to do. If you haven't earned the right, pushing is obnoxious. If you have earned the right, pushing will be interpreted correctly as caring. It's just that simple! Now, we're going to make it even simpler."

Joe laughed. "I can't believe you can make it simpler!"

DAY 13: CLOSING – PRECIPITATING ACTION

Brad took the fourth card, flipped it over briefly to show that this card was printed on both sides, and handed it to Joe, who scanned the front and read it out loud.

Third-Brother Action Step #33
(Closing 4 of 4)

Close with "Old Faithful"

Old Faithful is the only final close you'll ever need.
It can't be answered with a *"no"* and it's guaranteed to get the order... or get you closer if an order is possible.
In it's most basic form "Old Faithful" is:

"Are you ready to go forward, or do you still have questions?"

Brad then added, "Old Faithful is the close I mentioned earlier. It's the only final close you'll ever need. You can ask it a million different ways, but basically, you're asking the prospect to take the next step in the process—*or* tell you what questions need to be answered to take the next step.

"Let's look at a few examples on the back of the card."

Joe flipped it over and read the examples out loud.

(Closing 4 of 4, cont'd)
Old Faithful: Examples

★ Do you want to go forward with option 1 or 2, or do you still have questions?

★ If you have no additional questions, let's write it up.

★ Do you have any other questions before we write this up?

★ We've answered your questions. Let's look at the next step.

Joe shrugged. "Brad, these are all similar."

"That's true. They're all similar because they follow the same pattern. They all ask two questions: Are you ready to close—or do you still have questions? Remember, you're giving the prospect the option of a trial close or a final-Close. Pick a couple of versions you're comfortable with, practice them, and you're ready to close. Old Faithful will either get the order or get you closer to the order—*if* an order is possible. As I mentioned earlier, sometimes an order is *not* possible. For example, the prospect may not have the authority to make a final decision, or your competitor may be a close relative to the buyer. There are multiple reasons you might not be able to close, but Old Faithful is the best way to close or to surface objections that may still be hidden."

Joe interrupted. "Why would I want to surface more objections at this point?"

"Excellent question, Joe. If there *are* hidden objections and you *don't* uncover them, you're probably not going to close, and you may never know why. However, if you do uncover hidden objections, you'll at least have an opportunity to address them while you're still with the prospect and possibly even move the process forward to closure.

"I suggest you review both sides of this last card at least a dozen times before your call on TRB later today. Don't just read it silently to yourself; read it out loud. Words and actions crystalize in your brain when you read out loud. Besides, the written word and the spoken word aren't the same. The spoken word uses contractions and inflections. The written word sounds canned or fake when spoken. Practice out loud until you sound and feel natural.

"Okay, Joe, let's summarize the close. You earn the right to close by doing everything we've discussed to this point. Most bottom 96 percent salespeople think prospects will close themselves, but it's not true. Prospects aren't typically sitting in their offices hoping you'll stop in so they can give you an order. You must be prepared—you must earn the right

DAY 13: CLOSING – PRECIPITATING ACTION

to push, even if only gently. And then, use 'Old Faithful' to close or to tip the next domino in the closing process."

Joe marveled, "I've always thought closing was more complicated than that!"

"It's only complicated for the bottom 96 percent," Brad said. "For the top four percent, it's standard procedure. It becomes automatic when all the thinking, planning, and practicing becomes crystalized or programmed into their *mental and muscle* memory.

"Joe, I have a question. After your meeting with TRB this afternoon, how will you know if you've been successful?"

"It seems obvious—I'll be successful if I close the deal!"

"Okay, Joe, but what if you do everything according to your playbook and you *don't* close the deal? Does that mean you failed?"

Joe furrowed his brow. "Well, yeah. Sounds like failure to me."

Brad shook his head. "No! If you don't get the result you want, it's not failure. But if you don't prepare and give the call your *best effort,* that's failure! So, here's your assignment for tomorrow. In addition to making a successful sales call on TRB this afternoon, I want you to take twenty to thirty minutes immediately after your call to write a critique of your performance. Your critique should have two bulleted lists. One is for things you did that were good, and the other is for things you could have done to make the call better. Of course, if your call is perfect, there won't be anything on the second list."

Joe responded, "Yeah, right!"

Both men laughed.

"Tomorrow, we'll go into more detail about how to measure the quality of your sales calls, and we'll introduce the Universal Law of Sales Success."

Joe was intrigued. "Universal Law of Sales Success?"

As Brad stood to leave, he said, "Correct! It's a law that we discovered. It's kind of like the law of gravity that has always been with us but wasn't acknowledged until the late 1600s by Sir Isaac Newton. The

Universal Law of Sales Success wasn't acknowledged or recorded until the mid-1990s. That's when we made it part of our seventeen-day program. That's when we started applying it to our day-to-day operations. That's also when our results went from good to phenomenal. Again, we'll talk more about it tomorrow."

"That's it?" Joe asked. "Shouldn't I know more about this Universal Law of Sales Success *before* today's sales call?"

"Trust me, tomorrow will be the perfect time to introduce it. Tomorrow, we will also talk about measuring the quality of your sales calls.

"For now, trust me—you have everything you need to succeed in today's sales call. You've worked hard, and you're ready. You're going to be pleasantly surprised at how enjoyable it is to be in sales now that you are trained to *know* the best—and trained to *do* the best."

As Brad stood to depart, Joe, still a little apprehensive, smiled and nodded his admiration and appreciation for this new mentor in his life. Brad softly punched Joe's shoulder and gave him a thumbs-up. "Have courage! You'll do great!"

Day 14: Measuring Quality

5:30 a.m.

Joe walked into the diner with his shoulders back, wearing a new, well-fitted suit. Exuding confidence, he didn't feel the same as the day before. He greeted Brad with an upbeat "Good morning!"

"You're looking sharp," Brad said, smiling.

Sliding into his side of the booth, he replied, "Thanks, Brad."

"New suit?"

"It is," Joe affirmed as he unbuttoned his jacket. "You've been telling me to be my best, and I realized that involves more than what I say. It involves how I say it, what I wear, and the confidence I project. It reminded me of when I first started selling. I only had two suits. One didn't fit very well, but the other did, and it looked more professional. When I had an important appointment, I wore the nicer suit and even thought of it as my 'closing suit.' I always did better when I wore it.

"I thought about that yesterday after you gave me the assignment, and I decided it was time to upgrade my wardrobe, even before calling on TRB. So I went to a nearby men's store and bought this suit. You'll be proud to know I even used an Up-Front Contract to sell the store owner on doing the alterations by noon. I said, 'If you promise it'll be ready by noon, I'll pay cash.' He bought my cash and paid for it at noon with a new suit!"

Brad marveled at Joe's play on words as Joe continued, "Looking and feeling nice made a huge difference in my confidence when I called on TRB. You know, Brad, I think most salespeople in my company believe they're doing their best, doing what they've always done, saying what they've always said, and even wearing what they've always worn—and worst of all, thinking they're trained when they haven't really been trained. They appear to work hard but struggle to get results."

Pausing and looking down at his playbook, Joe said, "I struggled too! But now, I'm committed to being my best. And I realize this means making a lot of improvements. That's why I love the elegance and common-sense simplicity of your program. I really see myself growing into that top four percent. All that to say, thanks for the time you've invested in me, and thank you for this playbook. You're changing my life!"

Brad grinned, and his eyes welled up in response to the sincerity of Joe's words.

Joe waited a few seconds, then pulled out a handwritten sheet of notes. "Now, let's talk about my sales call and my assignment."

Brad sat back, waiting for Joe to continue. He couldn't help noticing how Joe was carrying himself—no longer the man he had met a couple of weeks earlier. Joe's upbeat attitude could be seen and felt. He was clearly more in control of every word and action.

Joe placed his notes on the table. It was one sheet of paper with two columns. *GOOD* was written at the top of the left column, and *BETTER* was written over the right column. Below each title were bulleted lists—five bullets in the left column and three in the right.

"Brad, before we dig into the assignment, I want to acknowledge that I still have a lot of work to do. I did my best in yesterday's sales call—I did everything you taught me. And I *did* make great progress! But I *didn't* get the sale!"

Joe leaned toward Brad and said in a quiet voice, "However, I'm sure you already know that." Brad's smile confirmed Joe's suspicions. Leaning back and speaking in a normal voice again, Joe added, "You know, after the meeting yesterday, they gave me a brief tour of the operation. As we returned to the lobby, I noticed a wall with framed pictures—

photos of past presidents and board members. As I'm sure you're aware, one face really caught my attention."

He took a deep breath and let out a sigh. "Brad, the face I recognized had a little plaque at the bottom with the inscription: 'Brad Roberts—CEO.'

"When I saw it, I was shocked, and I wondered why you hadn't told me."

Brad leaned his arms on the table. "It wasn't a secret, Joe. It just never came up in our conversation. When you said you had an appointment with TRB, I decided to let it play out to see how you would do with your training."

Joe's eyes widened in surprise. "So, it was a test?"

"Kind of," Brad confessed. "But it wasn't planned as a test; it just worked out that way."

Smiling again, Joe sat straight, opened his hands, and shrugged. "So, how'd I do?"

"You did really well. But let's talk about what happened during and after your call yesterday."

Joe looked up for a moment, gathering his thoughts. "Well, there were three people from TRB at the meeting. After introductions and some brief small talk, I used my planned questions and made good progress in finding several needs my company could fill. They seemed impressed with my focus on *their* needs and my desire to understand *their* goals. It was probably the first call I've ever made where I listened twice as much as I talked. In fact, the less I talked, the more excited they became and the more they opened up. They started treating me like I was an old friend! It was awesome.

"I didn't make a sale yesterday, but I did get an appointment to come back with a formal proposal when their board meets later this afternoon. It's their quarterly board meeting. I don't have a lot of time to prepare, but even so, the timing is good, and I'll be ready.

"I left the building, went to my car, and…" nodding toward his notes on the table… "immediately started working on the assignment."

Joe paused briefly and said, "The sales call was great, thanks to all your advice and preparation, so I hope you're proud of your newest protégé, even if I didn't close the sale."

"I *am* proud, Joe. But you're wrong! You *did* make the sale! You sold them on trusting you, and you sold them on having you attend today's board meeting. Tell me, what are you going to do with the two lists you created?"

Joe was initially surprised by the question. He thought Brad was going to tell *him* what to do with the two lists. He smiled and looked Brad in the eye. "If this is another test, I'm ready for it. I've already taken the good things and the things I could have done better and written them in the goals section of my playbook. They've already impacted my goals and planning for today's meeting. I've also set some longer-range goals for things I'm going to study and practice in the coming week."

Brad was seriously impressed. "You keep this up, and we may need to add a 'fourth-level brother' to the story! What else happened after the call?"

Joe leaned back and opened his hands. "When I got back to my office, I figured if you weren't going to tell me about your history, I would find out for myself. I dug deeper into your company online and found it started as Allied Applied Sciences. But then, thirty-five years ago, Allied changed its name to TRB, Inc.—Three Roberts Brothers! Brad, why didn't you say something sooner?"

"Like I said a few minutes ago, Joe. It wasn't a secret, but it was a great opportunity to see how you're progressing toward that third-brother, top four percent echelon.

"But before we go on, what else did your research into TRB reveal?"

"Well, Brad, the more I dug, the more I learned. I found an interview where you talked about how you and your two brothers took jobs at Allied Applied Sciences after college. The story you told about the three brothers was actually about you and your brothers! Most surprisingly, I found the third brother who saved the day wasn't you! In fact, the story implied you were the second brother. Is that true?"

Brad nodded and grinned sheepishly. "It's true. Joe, that was a turning point for me. I kept seeing my brother—the third brother in the story—getting promotions, making more and more money, and enjoying his daily work. For me, it was a daily grind, if you know what I mean."

"I do! Tell me more."

Brad continued, "Well, I was frustrated. So, I stepped back and looked at my work and my brother's work from a new perspective. My brother kept getting promoted because of his initiative. He always did *more* than asked or required, and he always followed projects through to completion—and beyond! I only did what was asked. Granted, it was more than our first brother, but I never thought past what I was told to do.

"One day, I decided to make a list of all the things my successful brother *did* that I was *not* doing. At first, I thought the list would be long, but the more I wrote, the more I realized there were only a few things he did differently. That was the beginning of me starting to act more like my successful brother—the third brother in the story. That was also the beginning of our learning how to measure the quality of a sales call.

"I realized measuring the quality of a sales call would be subjective—that is, subject to opinion. In other words, it would *not* be easy to measure. So, after listing the things my brother did that were better than what I did, I estimated my level of satisfaction with my performance for each thing on a scale from zero to ten. I started working on each area that was less than ten. Within a short time, my quality improved—at least in my opinion. Whether my opinion was right or wrong wasn't important. What *was* important were my *results*. They skyrocketed! That's when I realized that third-brother performance—doing more than asked or expected—leads to third-brother results.

"Our first brother turned things around as well, and the rest is history.

"My brothers and I bought the business when the founder retired, and we renamed it 'Three Roberts Brothers,' but then we shortened it to TRB. But enough about me and TRB."

Brad slid a new card across the table. As Joe looked down at it, Brad continued. "Several years ago, Joe, we discovered a basic law for success in sales. It revolutionized our approach to everything! We found the law to be universal. It applied to *all* forms of communication, *all* forms of persuasion, and *all* forms of selling."

"So, Brad, is this some kind of magical formula for sales success?"

Brad smiled but shook his head. "No, just the opposite! It's totally logical and so simple, it's amazing it wasn't discovered during the previous five thousand years of recorded history. We called it 'The Universal Law of Sales Success' and we first discovered it in the 1990s. The formula wasn't published until 2004.[2] And, it wasn't called the Universal Law of Sales Success until several years later.

"So, Joe, let's look at the law, and then I'll tell you why we believe it wasn't discovered sooner."

Placing the card in front of Joe, Brad recited it out loud from memory.

Third-Brother Action Step #34
Apply the "Universal Law of Sales Success"

Activity x Quality → Results
Activity Multiplied by Quality Yields Results!

You ***control*** your activity: what you do.
You ***control*** your quality: how well you do it.
These two things influence your results,
but... your prospect ***controls*** the results!

---

2 *Natural Selling Concepts*, P.171–173; © 2004, Be-Elite Publishing, ISBN 09745736-1-2

DAY 14: MEASURING QUALITY

"Notice it doesn't say 'activity multiplied by quality *equals* results'—it says *yields* results. The more activity you *do*—and the higher the quality of that activity—the *greater* the results will be.

"That's the Universal Law of Sales Success, Joe. We believe the reason it wasn't discovered or acknowledged earlier was because of another foundational law that was not revealed until the late 1970s. That's when W. Edwards Deming revolutionized manufacturing all over the world. He's credited as being among the first to recognize the importance of continuous process improvement. He's often quoted as saying, 'If you don't measure it, you can't manage it.'

"His statement is not only true for manufacturing; it's also true for everything you might ever want to manage. Deming and his protégés measured activity, results, and precise measurements for physical products that were being manufactured.

"Now listen carefully, Joe. This is critical! Deming measured physical, manufactured parts. He measured the results of the manufacturing process by measuring physical products. However, results are *not* proof of the *quality* of the sales call. Results can be *good* even if the salesperson does a poor job, and results can be *poor* even if the salesperson does a good job. We needed to be able to *measure* the quality of a sales call independent of results, and there were no systems in place before the mid-1980s to do it. We realized that if we were ever to measure the quality of a sales call, we would need to be able to measure the quality of human behavior.

"That's when we developed a system that allowed us to accurately measure subjective things like human behavior. We published our system in workbooks and started using it in our training. Eventually, our work inspired the development of the Universal Law of Sales Success. Prior to then, the quality of human behavior had always been considered *unmeasurable* because it's *subjective*!"

Joe interrupted, "You've said a couple of times now that the quality of sales calls is subjective. What do you mean, *subjective*?"

"When I say measuring human quality is subjective, Joe, I'm saying it's based on or influenced by personal feelings or opinions—it's not *objective*; it's subject to confirmation bias. That means we judge, or mentally measure the quality of human behavior based on our preconceived biases, and not based on logic or facts."

Joe's eyes betrayed his confusion. "You're losing me again, Brad."

"Let me give you an example, Joe. Consider measuring the quality of your eye contact. If your manager says the quality of your eye contact, on a scale of one to ten, is a five, would you agree?"

Joe felt uneasy but slowly answered, "I'd say it's closer to a nine. I think my eye contact is pretty good."

"Okay, you say nine on a scale of one to ten, but your manager says five. Who's correct?"

Joe smiled and said, "I hope I am, but honestly, I don't know!"

Brad enthusiastically acknowledged, "You're *both* right! From your perspective, it was a nine; from your manager's perspective, it was a five. You have different numbers because you have different perspectives—different confirmation biases! But here's the critical question, Joe, whose perspective really *counts* since you both have opinions that are subjective?"

"It's probably not safe to disagree with my manager," Joe said after pondering the question, "But I still think it's better than a five."

"Joe! *Neither* of your perspectives count! The only perspective that counts is the *prospect's* perspective. But here's the problem: prospects don't tell us how they feel about our quality. I've never had a prospect tell me my eye contact was good or bad. I've never had a prospect tell me I talk too fast or too slow. I've never had a prospect tell me I asked too many or too few questions. In over forty years of selling, I've never had a prospect *ever* comment on the quality of my sales call, other than the occasional comments like how they 'appreciate' me or my company.

"Let's face it," Brad tapped the card. "We control our quality, Joe.

But we can't know for sure that we're improving it without some sort of accurate system to measure it."

Brad reached into his briefcase and pulled out a new card. "Let me show you the system we developed and refined over the last three decades at TRB. This next card is a tool that allows you, and anyone shadowing you, to actually *measure* the quality of your call. It's called the Quality Measurement System™. We call it the QMS. It consists of fourteen short questions. It's two-sided, and it's the tool that has helped us—more than any other—to improve the quality of our sales calls.

"As you read this QMS card, Joe, I want you to notice that all fourteen quality questions relate to *your* quality. There's nothing in there about the economy, pricing, competition, or any other obstacle. Your success isn't determined by obstacles! Your success is determined by *you* and how you handle those obstacles."

Joe read both sides of the card to himself:

Third-Brother Action Step #35

Name: _____ Date: _____

QMS™ (Quality Measurment System)
On a '0' to '10' scale... **How was your:**

1. Preparation?	0 1 2 3 4 5 6 7 8 9 10
2. Introductions and start?	0 1 2 3 4 5 6 7 8 9 10
3. Enthusiasm?	0 1 2 3 4 5 6 7 8 9 10
4. Question quality?	0 1 2 3 4 5 6 7 8 9 10
5. Listening skill?	0 1 2 3 4 5 6 7 8 9 10
6. Ability to ID real needs?	0 1 2 3 4 5 6 7 8 9 10

> *Side 2*
> **QMS™ *(Quality Measurment System)... Continued***
> On a '0' to '10' scale... **How was your:**
> 7. Effectiveness with UFC's? 0 1 2 3 4 5 6 7 8 9 10
> 8. Listening? *(Listened more than talked?)* 0 1 2 3 4 5 6 7 8 9 10
> 9. Handling of objections? 0 1 2 3 4 5 6 7 8 9 10
> 10. Eye contact & Voice clarity? 0 1 2 3 4 5 6 7 8 9 10
> 11. Closing the next step? 0 1 2 3 4 5 6 7 8 9 10
> 12. Prospecting? 0 1 2 3 4 5 6 7 8 9 10
> 13. Summary of commitments? 0 1 2 3 4 5 6 7 8 9 10
> 14. Setting the next appointment? 0 1 2 3 4 5 6 7 8 9 10
> **Total:** _____ **Average:** _____

"How exactly does this work?" Joe asked.

Brad answered, "The theory behind the QMS is simple. If you have two subjective opinions and average them together, the new average will be more objective. If you have three subjective opinions and you average them, the new average will be even more accurate. If you take fourteen subjective measurements and average them, your new average will be exponentially objective. Essentially, you are making an individual's subjective opinion more objective with each additional opinion. Then, if you take two or three people and average all their opinions, the overall result is incredibly accurate.

"And by the way, Joe, fourteen isn't a fixed number of opinions to make the QMS work. We have some business partners who have modified it to include as many as fifty questions or opinions, and some to as few as ten.

"The number of questions or opinions isn't as critical as how often you use the system—it must be used consistently. The more you use it, the more accurate it becomes!

"Now, let's get back to you and what you need to do. It's important for you to review these fourteen questions *before* every sales call. It will be a great reminder before the call of what's going to be important during the call. Reviewing the list will put these things in the forefront of your memory, and you'll more likely remember them when the action starts. In fact, I recommend you put the card at the top of your notepad where you'll see it during the call, but not so conspicuous that it will distract other participants.

"After that, proceed to execute your agenda, asking your planned questions, followed by good active listening and follow-up questions. Continue in your call until you get an Up-Front Contract and close, or until you end the call. Whether you close or not, be sure to end by summarizing all commitments—yours and theirs—as well as the next steps! Before you leave, remember to set the next appointment date and time. The end of a sales call is the best time to schedule the next meeting. Your prospects will typically have their calendars close by."

Brad then took several used QMS cards out of his briefcase and laid them on the table. The used cards were covered with handwritten notes, and Joe's name was at the top of each.

"Even though I knew you were calling on our company yesterday, my three managers who attended your presentation were not aware that you and I know each other.

"Whenever my people meet with a new vendor, each of them completes a QMS card to measure the quality of the salesperson's preparation and presentation. A good professional approach tells them you're the kind of person who is prepared—the kind of salesperson they might want for a supplier or, 'business partners' as we prefer to call our suppliers.

"The notes and numbers you see handwritten on the cards are their comments and scores for each of the fourteen questions for your call yesterday. On the zero-to-ten scale, ten is excellent, five is okay, and zero is a bust. We know each score is subjective and only an opinion, but as I just said, when we took all the scores on all the cards and averaged them, the overall result was a more objective measurement of your quality. We used these individually subjective opinions—now made more objective—to evaluate you as a prospective business partner. Again, we see potential suppliers as future business partners, so we're very careful which we select."

Joe stared at the cards in amazement. "That's brilliant! You're always a step ahead of me."

Then looking up at Brad, he asked, "So, how'd I do?"

"Joe, you did great! I think you must have a wonderful teacher,"

They both laughed.

Joe scratched his head as he said, "I see how *you* use the QMS, but I doubt most of my prospects will want to fill one out, so how would your system help me measure the quality of *my* calls?"

Brad handed Joe the three completed cards. "These will give you a head start. You'll learn more about the quality of your sales calls from these cards than you'd learn in a year making sales calls without feedback.

"From now on, Joe, fill out your own QMS card for each sales call. Or if you make more than one call a day, you can wait until the end of the day and fill one out with your opinion of the average for the whole day.

"Additionally, once a month, use the QMS system with your sales manager, or possibly a coworker traveling with you to several sales calls. Afterward, have your manager or coworker score you on each of the fourteen questions. Fill one out on yourself as well, and then compare your scores with theirs. The places where your scores are different—like if you give yourself a nine in one area and your manager gives you a five—those are the areas you have a good reason to discuss. Whenever you and your manager have scores that differ by more than two points, you might have identified a blind spot! Keep in mind that your manager's score is always correct from their perspective—don't argue with their score. It's their *opinion* on what they saw. It's good to know because if your manager saw a three or four, maybe your prospect saw a three or four. It's a great way to *see* your quality through another person's eyes.

"After years of measuring thousands of sales calls, we've found the following guidelines to be remarkably consistent: A total score of 126 out of 140 is top four percent quality. Anything less is bottom 96 percent quality."

Joe quickly glanced at the results on the QMS cards from the previous day's sales call. His scores were all in the 110 to 115 range. "Kind of looks like I failed."

"Not so!" Brad exclaimed. "Considering how new this system is for you, your scores are awesome. Remember, 126 is top four percent quality, and you're not far from that. Plus, I know you have a follow-up call with TRB's board this afternoon, and I'm confident you'll do even better than your first meeting."

Brad pulled Joe's assignment sheet closer. "Your two-column self-evaluation was good. But now, I want you to add your QMS system. Between the two, you will more accurately measure and subsequently manage your sales call quality. Then use your self-evaluation and QMS cards to set goals—to become your best. You'll be in the top four percent before you know it."

Brad pointed to the three QMS cards. "I see our managers gave you nines and tens on the last four questions. Looks like you finished strong. That's terrific!"

"But, Brad," Joe protested, "I didn't complete the sale!"

"True, but you closed the next step *in* the sale—you're meeting with the board of directors later today."

Joe felt his confidence growing. "That's true, Brad. I did schedule a meeting to meet with the board—hopefully, to close. Your training over the last two weeks helped me build a solid agenda, taking the guesswork out of the process. It set me up to meet your board and created an opportunity for my firm and yours to both profit."

"Exactly. The teacher appeared because the student was ready."

Joe grinned. "I *am* ready, Brad. And I have *you* to thank for it."

Brad smiled and nodded. "You're very welcome, Joe. It's been my pleasure." He paused and looked at the time on his cell phone. "Unfortunately, I'm out of time today. Let's quickly look at your next assignment.

"I want you to do three things. First, list your goals for the upcoming TRB board meeting. Include the issues you still need to address to fill your parts of any Up-Front Contracts you have. Second, use your list to develop your agenda. Specifically, prepare the questions *you'll* ask, along with lambs—responses to the questions or objections you anticipate."

Brad scooted out of the booth and stood. "The third part of your assignment is to take a blank QMS card to every sales meeting, starting today! Have one in front of you in every call from now on as a reminder of the important things to remember *during* the call.

"Tomorrow, we will dig into follow-up, which I like to call follow-through. Follow-through is more than a thank-you, Joe. It's an essential skill for the top four percent." Brad dropped some money on the table to cover the bill. "Oh… and I'm looking forward to seeing you later today at our board meeting."

Joe stood and firmly shook Brad's hand. "I guess I'll see you later, then."

For the first time in fourteen days, they walked out together—not so much as teacher and student but more as friends.

As they walked out, Joe asked, "You said follow-up is more than a thank-you. More in what way?"

"Follow-*through*," Brad emphasized. "It's making sure you deliver more than you promise. You got your deal to the goal line; now you need to score. Tomorrow, we'll talk about an equally critical step: *delivery*. It's part of follow-through."

Joe stopped dead in his tracks. "Are you saying I got the order?"

Brad smiled but didn't answer. "See you later today, Joe."

Brad raised his hand to say goodbye and opened the door, the bells clanging. Joe's mind raced as he considered all that Brad had taught him. He changed his mind about leaving. He decided to work on his assignments while they were still fresh in his mind.

Day 15: Applying the Universal Law of Sales Success

5:30 a.m.

Joe walked into the diner ten minutes early and sat in their normal booth. Settling in with a cup of coffee, he reviewed his assignments from the day before.

Brad came through the door at five-thirty on the dot. Their server smiled at Brad and set a steaming mug on the table for him. Then he said, "I thought you might like to start your day with your usual order."

"Thanks," Brad said. "I need my caffeine."

The server continued, "I've been listening to some of your conversations, and I thought I'd act like a third brother."

Both Joe and Brad looked astonished. Smiling, Joe gave the server a high five, and the young man moved on to the next table.

"Good morning, Joe. That young fellow just made my day."

"It *is* a good morning, Brad. Signing that contract with TRB yesterday was awesome, and I have you to thank for it."

"You earned it, Joe. You opened a major account yesterday. How do you feel right now?"

Joe broke eye contact with Brad momentarily and said, "Actually, I have mixed emotions. I'm super-excited about the new business, but I don't feel like I'm anywhere close to the top four percent. Honestly, I just don't feel that much different than when we started."

Brad leaned over the table. "Joe, let me confirm your fears. You're *not* that much different."

Joe's eyes widened as Brad continued. "You're just doing important things a little better than before. All you need to do now is keep it up—keep doing things a little better every day—keep improving your best! Bottom line, Joe, continue focusing on being and doing a little better every day! You'll be a *top-four-percenter* before you know it."

"Okay, Brad, I sincerely appreciate the pep talk. But how's a *little* better going to get me into the top four percent?"

Brad acknowledged Joe's frustration with a gentle sigh. "Joe, have you ever been to a horse race?"

Joe was a little confused by the question. "Well, yes… I have, and I know you're about to make a point here, but I don't see where you're going with this."

Brad opened his hands and asked another question. "Have you ever heard of a photo finish?"

"Sure," Joe answered. "Those are the most exciting races."

Brad paused a moment, then explained, "Selling and horse racing have several things in common. First, there's only one winner. Second, the winner gets a nice reward. And third, the winner only needs to be a *little better* than everyone else. It's called the 'Slight-Edge Principle.'

"Did you know that in a recent Kentucky Derby race, the first-place horse won a little over $1.4 million, and the last-place horse, who finished twentieth, didn't even get a certificate of participation?

"Another question, Joe. How much faster did the first-place horse run than the twentieth-place horse?"

Joe shrugged. "I have no idea, but I'm assuming the winning horse was significantly faster."

"Good assumption." Brad said… "but wrong! The winning horse covered the mile-and-a-quarter track in a little over two minutes. The last-place horse—the one that finished twentieth—was only eleven seconds behind the winner. That's only a nine percent difference.

"So much for the last-place horse, Joe, but what about the second-place horse? At the same Kentucky Derby, the second-place horse—also known as the *first loser*—was twenty feet behind when the winner crossed the finish line. The announcer said, 'It wasn't even close!' But guess what? The second-place finisher was less than *a half second* behind the winner, which is only *one-third of one percent*.

"Wow! I never thought of it that way," Joe said.

"Okay, now let's apply the Slight-Edge Principle to you and your company. How much commission does your company pay when you finish second?"

Brad waited, but Joe's blank stare answered the question.

After a long pause, Joe responded. "I hate to think how many times I've been so close to winning new business and then lost it!" Then he grinned. "I get it! The lights are coming on!"

Brad affirmed Joe's response with a nod. "Your results might not show it today, Joe, but you're already knocking on the top four percent door."

Joe got excited! "I'm knocking on the door? Does that mean I've arrived?"

Brad laughed. "Not exactly, but you're getting close. All you need to do is stay committed to doing your best, and continually working to grow a little better every day."

Looking out the window at the dawning light, Joe shook his head, then turned back to Brad. "It's hard to believe we've covered most of what I need to know to reach the top four percent. We've only been meeting a little over two weeks, and you're saying I'm almost finished?"

"No, I'm saying you're almost starting! You're almost a top-four percent salesperson. So before you start celebrating, let's review your assignments from yesterday."

Joe opened his playbook to Day 14, turned it toward Brad, and slid it across the table.

Brad donned his readers and slowly reviewed each assignment. "This is excellent, Joe. I asked you to build a list of possible issues you might encounter in your meeting yesterday. I wanted you to anticipate possible roadblocks, so you wouldn't be surprised later when closing. Anticipating problems is one of the keys to a successful presentation. In fact, the greatest hockey player of all time was a professional anticipator. He wasn't the fastest skater or the best puck handler. But when asked what made him great, Wayne Gretzky responded, 'Other players skate to the puck, but I skate to *where* the puck is *going*.' Your preparation guided you to where the sale was going—so again, good job.

"Your list of anticipated questions and objections with answers and lambs is also excellent. You earned the business yesterday because you were ready for pretty much everything they asked.

"Your third assignment was to bring your QMS card to the meeting. You did that! I noticed you occasionally glanced at it during the meeting. Some salespeople get nervous referring to their notes or QMS cards, but you handled it professionally. How did *you* feel, having the QMS card and your other notes in front of you during yesterday's meeting?"

Joe quickly answered. "You know, Brad, as I wrote the anticipated questions, objections, and lambs, it reminded me of college when I crammed for an open-book test. I had the book and notes, but since everything was fresh in my mind, I didn't need them! I was able to focus on being brief and bright."

Brad nodded with satisfaction.

Joe continued his self-assessment. "The same was true for the QMS card. Having it in front of me gave me a confidence I hadn't felt before."

Brad pulled a three-by-five card from his pocket and laid it on the tabletop. Joe instinctively reached for it, but Brad stopped him. "Not so fast, Joe. This one's not for you. It's for me."

Brad flashed a proud grin and said, "It's my *agenda* for the meeting you and I are having right now."

Joe was surprised. "I don't remember ever seeing you use an agenda. Why today?"

"I always have an agenda," Brad said. "Even though I haven't called your attention to it, I always have one. Showing it today is my way of telling you I practice what I preach.

"At the end of every day, before I leave work, I take a few minutes to make an agenda for each of my next day's meetings. Then, like your lists of anticipated questions, objections, and lambs, I refer to my agenda whenever needed. But I have most of the information up here." Brad tapped the side of his head.

Joe smiled. "You never cease to amaze me, Brad. Out of curiosity, what else do you have on your agenda for today?"

"Excellent question. I keep my agendas simple—usually two to four bullet points."

Brad turned the card so Joe could read the handwritten notes. "I have three objectives on today's agenda. First, check on Joe's assignment. Next, cover today's lesson on the Universal Law of Sales Success. And finally, give tomorrow's assignment. We've completed the first bullet point. But before we go on to the next, I want to emphasize two suggestions for every sales call.

"First, like I mentioned yesterday, always bring a blank QMS card. Second, always bring your playbook. Keep your upcoming sales call agendas behind the Day 14 tab so they're always in the same place. You can take notes on your agenda or on a separate pad of paper—whichever you prefer. Then, after *each* sales call, review your notes and transfer your commitments and follow-up items to your calendar or to-do list. After that, you can safely remove the pages from behind the Day 14 tab and file them in your customer or prospect folders, where you'll have easy access for additional planning and follow-up."

"Don't you mean follow-through?" Joe said.

Brad smiled. "Oh, you're good!"

"I'm learning from the best," Joe said, grinning.

Without even needing to signal for more coffee, the server anticipated their need and brought the pot to their table. He filled their cups to the brim with fresh coffee, then moved quickly to his next customer.

"He's good, too," Joe said.

"Yes, he is! And his tip will reflect it! Let's move on... We've been talking about measuring quality, but now it's time to dive deeper into the Universal Law of Sales Success. We covered it on Action Step #34, but just as a reminder, the Universal Law of Sales Success is 'activity multiplied by quality yields results.' Remember, it doesn't *equal* results—it *yields* results.

"We also talked about measuring the quality of a sales call. Do you remember Deming's admonition... 'if you *don't* measure something, you can't manage it'?"

Joe's eyes widened. "Brad, you asked me that yesterday!"

"Repetition is a remarkable thing, Joe. Remember, it's how we program our brain to make excellent decisions."

Brad pulled out three new cards. The first card read:

Third-Brother Action Step #36
Measure Critical Activity
Professional Goal #1

Set and measure daily, weekly, and monthly goals for the primary activity that influences your results

Your primary activity in sales is:
Sales Calls: In-person, virtual, and telephone

"Joe, when we talked about goals back on Day 3, I stressed personal goals. We touched on vocational or business goals, but personal goals are the *reason* we work. *They* are the destination. Business goals are the vehicles we use to generate income so we can make the trip to this personal destination as quickly and comfortably as possible."

Brad paused, and Joe asked, "You're saying my primary activity is sales calls, so the *number* of sales calls is a critical goal?"

Brad nodded. "Exactly."

"So, what's the *best* number of calls to make?"

"Well, Joe there's not an exact number, but for most salespeople, the right number is about twice what they currently do."

They both smiled in agreement.

"Each business is different. You'll never go wrong if you ask your sales manager how many calls you should make and then work toward doubling what they tell you. Activity is critical! You control it. A good rule of thumb is to make as many calls as you possibly can, but it's critical to do so without lowering your quality."

The second card read:

Third-Brother Action Step #37
Measure Critical Quality
Professional Goal #2

At least once a month during your first year—and once a quarter thereafter—ask a coworker or manager to observe a few of your sales calls. Have them complete a QMS™ card with honest feedback on your quality. Then, discuss their comments. Do not disagree or argue. Just try to understand what they saw and heard and remind yourself: This might be what my prospect saw and heard.

"Joe, my experience tells me if you get feedback on your quality from a manager or coworker, you will grow a hundred times faster than if you get no feedback. If you have blind spots, by definition, you can't see them, so you need a third-party observer to point them out. Third-party feedback is essential. But you must solicit it, and you must be careful to *not* criticize or disagree with whoever is giving the feedback.

Remember, it's *their opinion* from *their* perspective. It can't be wrong if it's only their opinion. If you criticize or disagree with the feedback, you discourage future critical feedback, reducing opportunities to mitigate blind spots."

The third card read:

Third-Brother Action Step #38
Measure Critical Results
Professional Goal #3

Measure **Results** — They testify to the effectiveness of your ***Activity*** and ***Quality***. And they keep your business alive!

"This is worth repeating, Joe: We measure results because they testify to the effectiveness of our activity and quality—and they keep our business alive! Remember, you control your activity. Be sure to measure and manage what you do every day! You also control the quality of your activity. Always use the QMS card to measure and manage your quality. And one last reminder! Even though you do not control your results, you must *measure* your results to know the effectiveness of your activity and quality. Then adjust your activity and quality to optimize your results.

"Activity is the easiest thing to improve for most people. Most bottom 96 percent salespeople only make half as many sales calls as they should.

"Quality can take longer to improve. But the good news is, there's no upper limit to quality. The top four percent optimize their activity while striving to continuously improve their quality.

"A quick summary, Joe… Be sure to measure and optimize your activity… doing as much as possible in the time you have. But—and this is a big but—don't sacrifice your family or your personal goals in the process. Remember, *they* are your reasons for working in the first place.

"Next, measure and constantly improve your quality. Get third-party feedback using a QMS card like the one we discussed. And finally, measure your results so you can see where you might need to make adjustments to your activity, to your quality, or… both."

"Now, I have a question, Joe. You have all the reasons in the world to be happy about the progress you're making and especially, the big order you closed yesterday. That was a significant accomplishment. And it was a result of a lot of hard work. But when I came in today, you mentioned you were concerned about your progress. Do you still think you aren't making good progress toward the top four percent?"

Joe hesitated at first, uncertain, then he slowly responded. "It's kind of weird. I have mixed emotions. I feel good about the order—and I *do* feel good about my progress—but for some reason, I also feel a letdown. It's kind of like the day after Christmas. I can't explain it."

"Do you remember John Goddard," Brad asked, "the world's greatest goal accomplisher?"

Joe nodded. "Yes."

Brad closed Joe's playbook and slid it back over to him. "John Goddard had the same problem you're experiencing. After completing some early goals, he noticed they were often followed by discouragement. It made no sense. Then one day, he realized the feeling of letdown was created by the void left behind when an exciting goal was no longer on the horizon.

"While he worked to achieve a goal, he had something every morning to look forward to. When he achieved his goal, the anticipation and excitement were suddenly gone. He felt bad but, like you, he couldn't explain it. Once he realized it was the absence of an exciting goal, he decided to build his lifetime list so he would always have something to look forward to each day. He even set a goal to never again take time to fret about the absence of an accomplished goal.

"Joe, you accomplished a major goal yesterday. The thrill of victory was followed by that same kind of void. Whenever you accomplish a major goal, you should immediately revisit your other big-rock goals and refocus your energy on your next target. No matter how well those in the top four percent do, they always know there's more they can accomplish. They say to themselves, 'I can do better,' and then… they *do*!"

Brad paused, obviously concerned about something. Joe, sensing Brad's hesitation, asked, "Is everything okay?"

"Yeah, I just had a thought. These random thoughts come and go; some I embrace, and others I just let float on by."

Joe was a little confused by Brad's response. "What kind of thought?"

Brad folded his hands in his lap, gazed off into the distance, and then focused on Joe. "I was thinking how great it would be if everyone who starts our program would succeed like you have. I would love for everyone to do well. But that doesn't always happen. Remember the Pareto Principle?"

"That's the eighty-twenty rule—right?"

Brad smiled. "Right. It applies here as well. Unfortunately, only about twenty percent of the people who start our seventeen-day program complete it. Even so, most of the eighty percent who don't complete it did see significant improvement by applying what they *did* learn."

"Brad, the process seems straightforward and achievable. Why do so many fail?"

"Nobody has to fail, Joe, but most do. There are two reasons: lack of commitment and lack of consistency. You committed on Day 1, and you consistently completed your daily assignments. That's why you have succeeded so far. That's why I know you'll continue to succeed."

Joe added, "I'd like to take the credit, but it doesn't hurt having a great mentor."

Brad acknowledged Joe's compliment with a slight smile, then continued. "There's an old saying that it takes twenty-one days to establish a habit," Brad said, "but that's not true. It can take a day or a lifetime to establish a good habit. Unfortunately, you can also break a good habit or establish a bad habit in a single day. If you're consistent in keeping your commitments, there's almost no limit to what you can accomplish.

"Do you know the difference between a commitment and a promise, Joe? Have you ever thought about that?"

Joe hesitated as he considered Brad's question. "Aren't they kind of the same thing?"

"No, they're quite different. A commitment is something you do for yourself, and a promise is something you do for others in addition to yourself. Every day, I gave you assignments, and you committed to them. Your commitments took on special meaning because you made commitments to *me*! When you did that, they became promises. They gave you extra motivation.

"Remember on Day 4 of the program when you said, 'I have to confess, I almost slept in this morning, but I would have felt bad if I stood you up'? You didn't sleep in because you made *more* than a commitment to yourself—you made a promise to me.

"As we've gone through this program, Joe, your commitments have been important; your promises have been *more* important; and your consistency has been *critical*.

"You asked why so many fail. The answer is simple: *Most* never commit. Many who *do* commit never promise anyone, and some of those who *do* promise, lack consistency."

Brad paused while his coffee was being refilled. "Before we talk about tomorrow's assignment, let me finish today by sharing one additional item that's part of your activity and quality, but not typical of what you measure. It's *follow-through*... And it's especially important when selling a product or service that someone else in your company delivers!

"Listen carefully, Joe. Follow-through is *always* part of your job! The top four percent salespeople tend to make promises. If nothing else, they reassure their prospective buyers that the decision they're about to make will bring a positive ROI or some other benefit. *Top-four-percenters follow through!*"

"I see where you're going with this. When I make a sale, I can't walk away from my promise to the client. I need to make sure the people in my company do the same."

"That's right," Brad said. "When we were developing this program years ago, we found it's best to make at least two calls after every order—one soon after the sale to make sure everything is progressing according to plan, and another after completion to make sure we delivered on all our promises.

"In a worst-case scenario, you might find an unhappy customer when you call back. Statistics tell us only about one in ten people complain when they're disappointed. The other nine just never buy again. Yet all ten will speak negatively about you and your company with their friends, family, and acquaintances. Following through allows you to address those customers who have issues *before* they get too upset. It also allows you to prospect for additional business if they have no problems or, even after problems if they have been properly addressed. Most important, it helps build and protect your reputation!

"It might sound strange, but it can actually be a benefit to have a problem with an order—*if* you don't have too many. Properly addressing a problem often creates a more loyal customer than if you never had the problem in the first place. It's one thing to *say* you have quality people and service, but it's more *impactful* when you prove it."

At that point, Joe opened his calendar. "Now that you mention it, Brad, I think I'd better schedule a couple of follow-through calls."

Brad smiled as he signaled for their server to bring the check. "You really are a third-brother. Now, for your assignment.

"We've spent the last two weeks learning how to set goals, make plans, and use questions to help persuade people to make good decisions. Your assignment for tomorrow is to review your monthly and weekly goals. We first talked about these goals when we met on the Sunday after Day 4. Do you remember what I said might be the most critical habit you'll ever develop?"

Joe said, "Not only do I remember, but I've also been doing it! I review my goals at the end of every day. I review my weekly and monthly goals, then I check my calendar and confirm my plan for the next day. Initially, my daily review took from fifteen minutes to the better part of an hour. But within a few days, it only took a few minutes, just like you said. I'm not exaggerating when I say I'm getting more than twice the work done, and my work is more meaningful and more enjoyable."

"That's great! You know, it only takes a few minutes each day, and it's the best way to stay focused on what's important.

"Now, back to your assignment. After reviewing your monthly and weekly goals, I want you to make two lists, one for your current problems, and another for your current opportunities. We'll go over both lists in the morning and start wrapping up the program. See you bright and early!"

Day 16: Completing the Challenge—What Now?

5:30 a.m.

Joe reflected on the last two weeks of whirlwind activity and growth as he sat in their booth at the diner. For the second day in a row, he had mixed emotions. The day before, he was happy about getting a major order, but he was not looking forward to hearing Brad say, "We've completed the program." In his heart, Joe didn't want their journey to end—even if Brad said, "We've arrived."

Just then, Brad walked in carrying his briefcase. "Good morning, Joe!" he said, sliding into the booth. "Are you ready to bring this thing in for a landing?"

"Actually, Brad, I'm not," he said, feeling a little down."

Brad looked surprised as Joe hesitated, and then continued. "Meeting here every morning is a great new habit, and I love it! In fact, I think it's one of the best habits I've ever developed, and I don't want it to stop."

Smiling warmly, Brad said, "I'll admit, I've enjoyed it too, Joe."

Brad opened his briefcase and removed an expensive new leather binder. "This is to replace the vinyl binder I gave you earlier. I would have given it to you sooner, but it's only given to the top four percent."

Joe was immediately filled with excitement when he saw his name embossed in gold on the front cover. He could hardly believe it. "Brad, this is beautiful! Thank you, I really appreciate it. I promise to make you proud. I love your daily encouragement and how you hold me accountable for the assignments. I really don't want our meetings to end. Have I really done everything I need to do to get into that top four percent?"

"Hold on, Joe," Brad said, "we're not quite finished. We have more to cover."

"Really? I thought we completed the playbook and were about to wrap things up."

"Not exactly, Joe. Your playbook *is* a great tool, but it won't take you into the top four percent—or keep you there. You have to do that! No team ever wins a Super Bowl or a world championship because they have a great playbook. They win because they have a great playbook, *and* they do the work—they execute!"

Brad took a new card from his pocket and gave it to Joe, who read it out loud:

Third-Brother Action Step #39

Review and Update Goals
Yearly, Monthly, Weekly
And then, do the work... Daily

Organize:	Marshal Resources	Do the Work!
Plan:	Prioritize Next Steps	Do the Work!
Execute:	One Bite at a Time	Do the Work!

"Do you see a recurring theme?" Brad asked.

Joe raised his eyebrows. "Another trick question?"

"*You* have to do the work daily, Joe. Not me! People who rise to the top four percent are different. They *do* things differently. They don't settle; they do the demanding work. They're consistent, they organize, they plan, and most importantly, they execute.

"The point is, Joe, people in the top four percent live by the Universal Law of Sales Success. They know that activity multiplied by quality yields results. They take action! They *do* the work!

"They know this is a universal law that relates to everything in life. Think about it, Joe. The food you eat and exercise you do, multiplied by the quality of your food and exercise, will yield, to a great extent, a *result,* which is the body you now occupy.

"The books you read multiplied by the quality of those books also yield a result, which is the wisdom and intelligence you now possess. This affects the quality of every decision you make and further impacts the quality of your future decisions. It's simple, yet profound."

Joe placed his old vinyl playbook next to his new leather binder. Then, motioning toward his older playbook, he said, "Brad, this program has literally changed my life. You've given me the tools I need to win. You also showed me how to optimize my activity and improve my quality. Basically, you've taught me to work smarter and harder, and you've taught me to strive to get better every day!"

"Excellent, Joe. I think you're ready for the final lesson. But first, let's look at your assignment from yesterday. I asked you to review your monthly and weekly goals and make two lists. A list of your current problems and a second list of your current opportunities."

Joe nodded. "I did that." He slid a few loose pages over to Brad. "I listed the opportunities and problems I anticipate for next week. Doing that, I felt the same knots in my stomach I had when listing all my goals back during our first week. But after about five minutes, the knots loosened. I ended up with fifteen opportunities and twelve problems.

"You know, Brad, for years the sales books and trainers have said, 'Problems are opportunities in disguise.' If that's true, then I have no problems—only opportunities. Do you agree?"

Brad shook his head empathically. "No, I don't! I believe when managers say problems are opportunities, they're really saying they don't have a solution. It might change the focus of the conversation from the problem to the solution, but that's about all it's good for. The problem still exists! Problems slow you down when you *don't* address them… Opportunities speed you up when you *do* address them."

"Wait a minute!" Joe protested. "Aren't opportunities and goals the same thing?"

"Not exactly. You could say, 'Opportunities are the steppingstones or to-dos, but they're hardly ever the goal."

Joe rested his elbows on the table. "You're losing me, Brad. Please tell me the difference between opportunities and goals."

"Okay. You just made a presentation to TRB. Your presentation was not the goal; rather, your presentation was an opportunity—a steppingstone on your way to the goal. Getting a signed contract was your goal.

"Here's another example. Sir Edmund Hillary wanted to climb Mount Everest. That was his goal. However, he had to complete hundreds of steppingstones along the way. These steppingstones, or action steps, were called problems when they slowed his progress, and opportunities when they speeded it up. So, when he came to an unplanned and uncrossable crevasse, he had a problem. He was prevented from moving forward until he sent for lightweight aluminum ladders that could be used as makeshift bridges.

"On the other hand, as part of his planning, he took advantage of opportunities by arranging for local Sherpas to stage supplies at several progressively higher base camps. His climb was accelerated by not having to carry extra food and oxygen bottles; they were already strategically placed along the route.

"Here's the point, Joe, once Hillary set the goal to reach the summit, he started seeing multiple opportunities and problems. Listing them did not make the climb harder; rather, listing both opportunities and anticipated problems prepared him to succeed. And he *did!*

"Hillary's goals were different from yours, but the process he used is similar to what you're doing to move into the top four percent. Hey, I just thought of something. Grab the card from Day 4—the one with the building."

Joe pulled a small leather pouch from his pocket. Opening it, he removed all the cards Brad had given him over the preceding two weeks.

"Nice organization, Joe, and a nice leather case. I'm impressed."

Smiling, Joe quickly located the card with the building and read it:

Pointing to the card, Brad continued. "Hillary set a significant goal, then he planned the best way to climb. He studied and trained himself in mountaineering, so he could do it proficiently and safely. He organized and executed. Then he ended each day by planning the next. That way, he could take the best advantage of opportunities, such as breaks in the weather.

"Hillary anticipated problems and marshaled the supplies he would need. He acquired special ropes, shoes, clothing, tents, oxygen bottles, and other equipment. These helped him tackle legitimate constraints and obstructions like crevasses, cliffs, and ice walls in real-time. He had to be flexible but often had to respond quickly—much like you do when you encounter an objection to your sale.

"Hillary's planning gave him the necessary time and margin to deal with unexpected obstacles when they arose. Do you see the parallel here?"

Joe cracked a smile. "I do!"

"You're already climbing, Joe. Your assignment to list and prioritize problems and opportunities is one of the last steps. Do you remember that Sunday we met?" Brad said. "I told you that within two weeks, you'd have everything you needed to get into the top four percent. Well, we're almost at the summit. We're almost ready to plant the flag!"

Brad reached out with his palm up. "Can I borrow your card pack for a minute?"

Joe handed the leather pouch to Brad, who quickly opened and removed the deck of neatly organized cards. He removed the Action Step #12 card and placed it in front of Joe. "Look at the third and fourth questions."

Joe read the two questions out loud. "Number three says, 'What opportunities exist for me to make progress?' and number four says, 'What obstacles do I anticipate?'"

Joe then looked up, his eyes telling Brad that more lights were coming on.

Brad continued. "Remember when I said, 'Goal setting, planning, and organization are a waste of time if you don't execute?' That's why it's important to take a few minutes at the end of each day to refocus. This doesn't mean rethinking and replanning everything. It means you briefly look at your goals and then take existing opportunities and obstacles into account as you plan your next day."

"OK, Brad, yesterday, you mentioned follow-up—sorry! I meant *follow-through*—so, I assume my top opportunity today is to make follow-through calls on the contract I just wrote."

"Actually, Joe, those are good things for today's to-do list, but they may not be today's biggest opportunities."

Confused, Joe said, "A week ago, on Sunday, we talked about monthly and weekly to-dos; now you're talking about daily to-dos. So, how do I prioritize *daily* to-dos?"

"Your promises will always be the top priority on your to-do list.

Everything after those should be rank-ordered based on the ROI of the task."

Raising his eyebrows, Joe asked, "The Return on Investment of the *task?*"

"That's right. Every task you undertake—every action—requires an investment of time, energy, and possibly other resources. When you're evaluating the priority of your daily to-dos, always ask yourself, 'Which will bring the greatest return or result compared with the effort or investment of time, energy, and resources?' Then, build your daily to-do list to optimize ROI for that day.

"Remember, to-do items are action steps or small tasks that add up to big accomplishments. They're the steppingstones to your goals. You'll find they can typically be accomplished in a single time block or less. Do you recall back on Day 4, we talked about using the system we call time-blocking?"

"Sure!" Joe responded, "I time-block my schedule every day."

"That's excellent, Joe. Now a key decision you should make at the end of each day is how you'll get the most out of the next day. That's why you do an end-of-day review of your opportunities, anticipated obstacles or problems, and goals. Then you prioritize your steppingstones and adjust, if necessary, your time blocks for the next day—highest priority first.

"You may not get everything done every day by using this system, but you *will* be focusing on the most important things. That way, you'll end each day knowing you worked on the highest priority and highest ROI tasks."

Joe took a deep breath. Every piece of the process was falling into place.

"Let's summarize where we are in the program," Brad said. "Then I have another assignment for tomorrow."

Joe felt reenergized at the thought of meeting with Brad again the following morning.

Brad signaled for fresh coffee. Then he opened his hands. "Actually, we can summarize the program in two short minutes."

Suddenly feeling confused, Joe said, "Excuse me?"

"Listen. You started your journey by learning to make excellent decisions as automatically as possible on the first two days. On the third day, you learned to set and prioritize personal and professional goals and to review them regularly.

"On the fourth day, we covered time-blocking and managing the activity you put into the time you have. Then, on the fifth day, we talked about thought–habit–action patterns. Those are the patterns we program into our brains to make consistently automatic, excellent decisions.

"Next, on the sixth day, we applied what we learned to the most important skill in selling. Do you remember what that is? It's also the most important skill in communication."

Joe didn't hesitate. "You mean asking questions?"

"Awesome! You answered with a question. You're correct. And once again, proof that you're becoming a third-brother."

"We spent some time developing the skill of asking *best* questions, because it's the most important skill in selling and in persuasion. And by now, Joe, you should realize it's the most important skill in communication, which makes it the most important skill in life. More about life skills tomorrow, but let's get back to our summary.

"After we talked about the importance of questions, we started creating your personal playbook on the seventh day and built it one day at a time. At first, it was a few cards and a pile of papers. Before you knew it, you were well on your way to having everything you needed to join the top four percent of salespeople.

"On the eighth day, we examined the best way to make the first call and the best way to build rapport and relationships. On the ninth day, we looked at the best way to use product knowledge to identify real needs. On the tenth day, we looked at the best way to use UFCs—Up-Front Contracts—which is the best way to qualify prospects.

"We learned the best way to give a presentation on the eleventh day, which is basically filling in your half of the Up-Front Contract. This was followed with the best way to handle objections on the twelfth day. That's when you created lambs for each of the eight types of objections you might get.

"Then, on the thirteenth day, we learned the best way to close or precipitate action. And on the fourteenth day, we learned about measuring sales call quality and introduced the Universal Law of Sales Success. That brought us to yesterday, our fifteenth day, when we dove deeper into the application of the Universal Law and the importance of good follow-up.

Joe interrupted, "Don't you mean *follow-through*?"

Brad grinned. "Hey! Who's teaching here?" His shoulders shook as he laughed. "The third-brother is becoming the teacher!"

Brad smiled and pushed out of the booth. "Joe, that concludes our summary. You now have everything you need to climb the ladder to the top four percent. Tomorrow, we'll talk about making sure your ladder is leaning against the best wall."

Joe felt confused. "Best wall?"

"That's right, Joe! The *best* wall. There's an old parable that says most people are on the broad road to failure, and only a few are on the narrow road to success. Many of those people on the broad road climb the ladder of success all their lives, only to realize it has been leaning against the wrong wall. Tomorrow, we're going to talk about how you can be sure your ladder is leaning against the *best* wall.

"Between now and then, think about what wall you want to lean your ladder against. What lasting result do you want for your life? What do you want to be remembered for?

In other words, Joe, when you reach the top of the ladder, what will be your legacy? What impact will your life have made on others after you're gone?

"That's what we'll talk about tomorrow. See you in the morning."

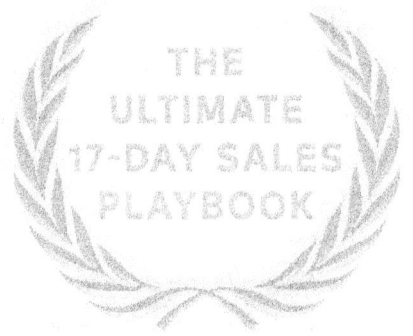

Day 17: Reaching True Top Four Percent Success

5:30 am

Joe arrived a little earlier and instinctively ordered two cups of coffee. He knew Brad would be there in the next few minutes. He was excited and confident, knowing he had everything he needed to move into the top four percent—and *stay* there.

Just then, hearing the bells, Joe looked up to see Brad walking in with a big grin on his face. "Joe, how's it going?"

"It's going well, but just like yesterday, I'm not looking forward to my mornings without you."

As their coffee arrived, Brad opened his briefcase and retrieved a small brown rectangular package. Pushing it toward Joe, he said, "I got you a little something to remind you of our time together. Please, go ahead and open it."

Joe's eyes widened in surprise. "Thanks! I didn't expect a gift. You've already given me so much!"

He carefully unwrapped a photograph of an old museum painting. He didn't recognize the man in the portrait. At first, he thought it might be a young George Washington, but centered at the bottom of the small, nicely framed picture was the sentence, "Activity multiplied by quality yields results."

He looked at Brad. "Is this the guy who invented the equation?"

"No. Actually, we were the first to write the formula in its current format.[3] But he applied it long before we wrote it. You may not recognize him in this photo. He's one of the most famous composers of all time. He published over six hundred works of music in his short life. He died at age thirty-five. Wolfgang Amadeus Mozart."

Joe shook his head slowly, obviously surprised. "Wow, I had no idea Mozart died so young!"

"This photo is not to compare you with Mozart; it's to remind you to stay focused on your highest priority activities each day and constantly improve the quality of your daily activities. There *is* a limit to how much you can do in a day, Joe. But, as I've said before, there's no upper limit to your quality.

"Mozart didn't invent the piano or violin, nor did he invent musical notes. But he did use them to compose music that the world still enjoys. He used tools that others created to achieve greatness—to leave his legacy.

"So from now on, Joe, whenever you look at this picture, I want you to remember that Mozart had the same number of hours in a day as you do. And, just like you, his results were directly proportional to the activities he put into his hours—and the quality of those activities."

"Putting activities into hours sounds odd to me. I normally think in terms of the hours I put into my activities."

"That's the problem, Joe, *and* the point! Most people spend their whole lives trying to manage their time. Do you remember what we said about managing time?"

"I do—you said the goal is to get more and higher quality activity into your time—not spend more time on your activity."

"That's right, and here's my point," Brad leaned his elbows on the table. "You created your playbook as we went through this program... *Now*, continue using it daily! Use it to change your future for the better. Strive to be consistent in your activities. Strive to continuously improve your

---

3 *Natural Selling Concepts*, © 2004, Be-Elite Publishing, ISBN 09745736-1-2 P.171–173

quality. And strive to follow your playbook, constantly polishing it as you go forward. Do these things, and you'll *always* be in the top four percent!"

Joe reflected on Brad's words for a moment before he spoke. "Are you saying my playbook holds all the keys for my success in life?"

"No. This book might be an important guide, but it's not the ultimate guide to a successful life. You're on the path to achieving excellent results because of it. But now let's talk about the purpose of those excellent results—a successful life.

"That's why yesterday, I said we would talk about your ladder leaning against the 'best wall.'"

Joe acknowledged: "I've been thinking about what that could mean since yesterday."

Brad handed him a new card. He read it out loud slowly:

Third-Brother Action Step #40

The Ladder of Success

Make sure your ladder is leaning against the best wall

"Some people spend their whole lives climbing the ladder of success, only to find, once they reach the top, the ladder is leaning against the wrong wall!" — Thomas Merton

---

Studying the card for a few more seconds, Joe felt puzzled and hesitant to speak. Then he said, "Brad, I'm not sure if I should feel good or bad. Are you saying my goals are wrong?"

Shaking his head, Brad replied, "Not at all! Your goals are *your* goals. Do you remember talking about your personal and professional lifetime goals back on our third day together?

"There were seven cards—one for each of the seven categories of goals. But only one card related to your professional life. The other six related to your personal life. Those personal goals are the only reason you even have professional goals—the only reason you work. Your personal goals are infinitely more important than your work goals. And I'll prove that mathematically in the next few minutes."

Joe's face expressed doubt. "Mathematically?"

Smiling, Brad said, "Stay with me. Today could be the most important day in our whole program. Let's get back to the ladder illustration. We use it to emphasize the most common mistake people make in their pursuit of success.

"Many people build temporary happiness by climbing fast and far. However, only a few seem to achieve permanent lifetime happiness.

"Your goals aren't wrong, Joe, *if* they're pointed in the right direction and *if* they're properly prioritized. In other words, your goals are good if the ladder you're climbing is leaning against the best wall and your priorities are right.

"But therein lies the problem. Most people *over-prioritize* work or vocational goals and *under-prioritize* important personal goals. This typically results in miserable, lonely, workaholics wondering where they went wrong and why they never feel satisfied."

Joe looked down, then back up, and slowly shaking his head, acknowledged, "That's kind of sad, isn't it?"

Brad nodded. "Yes! Sad but true! Technically, your life will probably last seventy to ninety years. Eternity is somewhere *way, way* beyond seventy to ninety trillion years. Our minds can't even grasp eternity.

"If you believe this life is all there is, then you have nothing to worry about—and nothing to lose—unless you're wrong! However, if you believe there may be more than just this life, then it makes total sense to search for answers to ensure you're prepared.

"I believe in life after death, Joe. I believe each person will spend eternity in heaven or in hell—in paradise or in torment. I also believe that eternity is a long time to be wrong. So it's important to get it right while you still have time.

"Your challenge, Joe, is to prepare for—and live—your best earthly life while simultaneously preparing for an even better eternity. Your challenge is to make sure your microscopic, earthly life is lived well as you prepare for eternity. Your challenge—as you live this current life—is to make sure your ladder is leaning against the best wall."

Joe looked down at his binder, seriously considering Brad's words. Then he made eye contact and asked, "Tell me, Brad, how did you make sure your ladder was leaning against the best wall?"

"At first, it wasn't. Remember, I was the second brother. But even after I became a third-brother, my ladder was still leaning against the wrong wall. I was on the road to workaholism. I didn't realize I was living to work instead of working to live. I know it's a cliché, but in my life, it was true.

"My ladder leaned against the corporate wall—the self-actualization wall—the *wrong* wall. The critical things in life, like family and health, were sacrificed on the altar of accomplishment. If you've ever seen *A Christmas Carol* by Charles Dickens, you know what I mean. I was a young Scrooge—rapidly becoming an old Scrooge!"

"You're not that person now," Joe said, shaking his head in disbelief. "If you were, you wouldn't be helping me. What made you change?"

Brad smiled. "I believe God sent an older man into my life—someone who took an interest in me and didn't pull any punches when I made mistakes and needed correction. He encouraged me to make wise decisions when working on business goals. He urged me to always focus more on my personal goals because those were my reason for business goals. He taught me to better understand other people by asking more questions and then, equally important, by listening to their answers. He also taught me to better understand myself by being introspective and questioning myself, always looking for improvement. He taught me to make wise decisions by preparing and asking *best* questions. And he taught me there's only *one best way* to do anything.

"Sound familiar, Joe?"

"Yes, it does!" Both men smiled.

Brad signaled for more coffee from their regular server.

"Yesterday, you asked me to think about what I want to be remembered for—what lasting impact I want my life to have after I'm gone. Is that why we're talking about making sure my ladder's leaning against the right wall?"

"Not just the right wall, Joe—the best wall."

Brad motioned toward Joe's binder. "Let's look at where we are and where we're going. This playbook contains everything you'll need to achieve top four percent performance."

Then, pointing to Joe's forehead, he continued. "You have everything up there to make sure you're happy with the result. You also have everything up there to make sure your ladder is leaning against the best wall."

Brad paused for a moment and then pointed at Joe's heart. "That's where true happiness lives. Happiness in this lifetime and happiness for the next seventy to ninety trillion years and beyond."

As the coffee arrived, Brad slowly and seriously said, "What I'm about to say is the most critical part of the program, so I need to reiterate several things.

"You have seven categories of goals: physical, social, mental, spiritual, financial, family, and vocation. The first six are personal, and the seventh category only exists to help you accomplish the first six.

"Your personal goals require thoughtful planning. The seventh category is your vocation, your business. It also takes thought and planning, but most people spend ten times more effort planning the less important seventh category than the other six combined. In fact, most people spend more time planning their vacations than their future. That's why I use the ladder illustration.

"Yesterday, I asked you to consider the following questions: What wall do you want to lean your ladder against? What lasting result do you want for your life? What do you want to be remembered for? When you reach the top of your ladder, what will be your legacy? What impact will your life have made on others after you're gone?

"So let me ask you, what have you decided?"

Joe thought for a few moments and then answered, "Those are tough questions, Brad. Before yesterday, I had never thought about my life that way."

"And now?" Brad smiled.

Joe opened his new, organized leather binder to today's tab. He flipped the tab over, exposing several neatly typed pages.

"Well, I wasn't sure where to start, so I decided to look up the last words spoken by a few famous people. I found some interesting quotes."

Joe read from his notes. "Alfred Hitchcock's last words as he lay on his deathbed were 'One never knows the ending—one has to die to know exactly what happens after death.' Sir Winston Churchill's last words were, 'I'm bored with it all.'"

Joe took a drink of coffee and continued. "As Benjamin Franklin lay dying at the age of eighty-four, his daughter suggested changing his position in bed so he could breathe easier. Franklin's last words were, 'A dying man can do nothing easy.'"

With one eye half closed and a confused look on his face, Brad asked, "Where are you going with this, Joe?"

"The people I mentioned each left a legacy. Hitchcock wrote stories that are classic—and then he died. Churchill became one of the greatest world leaders of all time—and then he died. Benjamin Franklin helped establish one of the most successful countries the world has ever seen—the United States of America—and then he died. They *all* died. Each left a legacy. And that's what I thought I wanted."

"That's what you wanted—past tense? But you don't want it anymore?"

Joe acknowledged the seriousness of the question by answering slowly, "Well, yes! I want to leave a legacy, but now I'm hearing you say there's something more important."

"That's exactly what I'm saying. Now, what do you think that 'something' is?"

Deep in thought for a moment, Joe guessed, "Lifetime happiness?"

Brad leaned back and smiled. "Mozart and the men you mentioned each left a legacy, but there's little evidence that any of them died happy. They contributed to the world and made it better. But to my knowledge, there's no evidence any of them felt happy or fulfilled. Wouldn't you agree that's a sobering thought?

"So, what's the answer, Joe? What impact do you want your life to have after you're gone?"

"I want to leave a legacy, but I also want people to say, 'He lived a full life and died happy and was looking forward to eternity'!"

"When we first met, Joe, I asked you a question. Do you remember what it was?"

"You asked, 'What's the problem?' I must have looked pretty miserable. And now that I think about it, I *was* pretty miserable."

"That's right," Brad said, smiling. "And what *was* the problem?"

"*I* was the problem!" Joe acknowledged sheepishly.

"Right again. But now you have a plan—a playbook—and you are no longer the problem. You'll never be the problem again unless you stop doing the activity, or you stop improving your quality, or you lean your ladder against the wrong wall!

"When you sat in this very booth the day we met, you were slouched over, feeling dejected. Your sales were down, and you thought, 'If only my sales were better, I would be happy with my job and my life.' Is that close?"

Joe grimaced. "Not only close; you nailed it."

"I've known plenty of people who had great sales, business success, and wealth, but they were miserable, and some still are. Why?" Brad asked.

Half-kidding, Joe responded, "Well, if I get wealthy, I'll be happy!"

Brad acknowledged Joe's humor with a quick smile, then continued to probe. "Listen carefully. The purpose of our program has been two-fold. The first was to show you how to get into the top four percent of your sales organization. Have we done that?"

"Absolutely! What's the second purpose?"

Brad took a deep breath. "The second is to show you that even if you achieve your vocational goals, you can still feel empty—you can still be unhappy."

"So, Brad, your objective for these last couple of weeks was to help me achieve a goal just to show me it isn't what I was looking for?"

Brad acknowledged Joe's clever play on words with a half-smile. "Well, I used to think achieving sales goals was the top of the mountain. And truth be told, vocational goals are important, but again, they don't bring lasting happiness. In fact, your comment about having wealth reminded me of myself. I thought I'd be happy after high school, then college, then after the new job, new promotion, new home. I completed each of those objectives, but the excitement of achieving them never lasted. Can you identify with that?"

Joe nodded in agreement.

"When I achieved certain things, it felt good for a while, but the feeling never lasted. So I kept writing and rewriting my goals. Finally, it hit me. Happiness doesn't come from having or doing things; it's the feeling that comes from knowing you're making progress toward your purpose in life."

Silence settled between the two men, despite the increasing noise in the diner and the city awakening around them.

Brad leaned in. "Do *you* know *your* purpose?"

Joe pondered the question, but he didn't know the answer.

"I respect you for not responding right away. It's a hard question. It's a personal question. But it's a critical question. I challenge you to search for the answer."

"Can't you just tell me?" Joe asked.

Brad smiled warmly, with a light in his eyes. "No, I believe the answer will affect your eternity. But only God knows what He has planned for you."

"Is this where you get all religious on me?" Joe asked, remembering how Brad always carried his Bible.

Brad laughed. "I hope not. I never cared much for Bible-thumpers, Joe. And I certainly don't want to be one. But having said that, I do have a little something for you."

Brad retrieved a second package from his briefcase. It was a small box with the word "Bible" printed in large letters across the front.

"Over forty years ago, the older man I mentioned challenged me to start reading the Bible. I told him I didn't really believe all that religious stuff, but he encouraged me to read just a small part of it. I can still remember his exact words. He said, 'Brad, if you're half as intelligent as I think you are, you'll not reject the Bible until you at least check it out.'

"Then he told me, 'Go to the index and find the book of John. It's a fairly small part of the New Testament.' He suggested I pray and ask God to reveal himself to me as I read it.

"Honestly, Joe, I thought he was a little crazy, but all his other advice had been excellent. So, out of respect and because I knew he had my best interests at heart, I told him I would."

Joe interrupted. "So he had earned the right to *push* you?"

Brad nodded slowly. "He did!

"So, later that evening, I prayed and started reading the book of John. Without really noticing when it happened, my life started changing. Within a few weeks, I began to understand who Jesus was—and is. My life has never been the same. Several years later, my wife gave me the little Bible that you see me reading each morning. It's like the one my son BJ reads. And it's like the one I just gave you. I read mine every day and try to follow God's wisdom in every decision I make. It's amazing how much better my days go. For instance, meeting you. That's a good example of what I mean—meeting you and starting this journey together.

"I can't prove it to you, but I believe if you accept my challenge to pray and read the book of John, one day you will be convinced of who Jesus is and how essential he is to earthly and eternal happiness. For now, I just ask you to trust me. This book showed me where my lifetime happiness wall was located. It showed me where the top of my earthly ladder should be leaning. It showed me how to live a full and happy life. It showed me that I will, in God's timing, be ushered into an even better—and even happier—eternity.

"Just like every other assignment in this program, Joe, it's optional. But I hope you'll do it."

Brad slid the Bible over to Joe and said, "Now, for the balance of our time today, I have two more things to discuss."

"Before you do, thank you for the picture of Mozart and for the Bible. I promise to work on this last assignment."

Then, in one of those rare moments that are forever etched in memory, Brad said, "Thanks, Joe. I value your promise, and I appreciate being part of your journey to true success. I have faith that you'll find your best wall. I'm praying that when you do, you'll lean your ladder against it."

Brad sat tall. "Now, back to the two things we still need to discuss.

"First, TRB is planning to announce later today that I'm retiring after our next board meeting. Brad Junior is retiring from the Air Force and will be taking over as CEO in my place.

"Second, we would like you to consider joining our board of advisors. We feel your newly demonstrated commitment to excellence and your ability to ask awesome questions will be a real asset to TRB."

"Wow, Brad—that's a real compliment!"

"I'll send you more information about the position when I get to the office. Look over the description and compensation and let us know if you have any questions. We typically meet for about three hours on the last Wednesday evening of each quarter to review progress and plans. If you choose to join us, your commitment shouldn't negatively impact your current employment or time with your family. After you review the information and ask any questions you might have, let me know your decision."

"I'm honored you would consider me for such an important position. Does this mean we will still meet regularly in the future?"

Brad grinned. "Yes, and no!" Joe's smile briefly disappeared, then returned as Brad explained. "I will not be attending most future advisory board meetings. We want BJ and the other managers to feel the freedom to make new decisions and take the company in new directions. Of course, I'll still see BJ, probably more than he wants. But it will be *his* company, and I know he's ready for the challenge."

"Okay, Brad, that sounded like 'no,' but I think I heard 'yes,' to possibly meeting in the future." With a big smile, Joe asked again, "Will we keep meeting?"

"That's kind of up to you, Joe. I'm usually available for coffee in the morning, and now that I'm going to be retired, I'll be available for telephone calls and occasional lunches—assuming you're buying." He laughed. "After all, I'll be unemployed."

Joe joined Brad in laughter. As they stood and shook hands, Brad added, "If you ever want to talk about the Bible or if you have any questions, I'm available. Promise me you'll call."

"You can count on it!"

Brad pulled a new Day 17 tab out of his briefcase and handed it to Joe. "This is a copy of my Day 17 tab. Have a look, and remember you promised to call."

After Brad left, Joe sat down again, contemplating what had just happened. He felt excited knowing he and Brad would continue as friends long into the future. Picking up the new Day 17 tab, Joe turned it over to find a personal note handwritten above two passages from the Bible…

"Joe, work to live. Do not live to work! The most important things in life happen before and after work. They can be recorded in a book, but they must be written on your heart. It's critical to always remember this."

Your friend always, Brad

Bible passage #1: How I work

"Whatever you do, work heartily, as for the Lord and not for men." Colossians 3:23

Bible passage #2: Why I work

"If I speak in the tongues of men and of angels, but have not love, I am a noisy gong or a clanging cymbal. And if I have prophetic powers, and understand all mysteries and all knowledge, and if I have all faith, so as to remove mountains, but have not love, I am nothing. If I give away all I have, and if I deliver up my body to be burned, but have not love, I gain nothing. Love is patient and kind; love does not envy or boast; it is not arrogant or rude. It does not insist on its own way; it is not irritable or resentful; it does not rejoice at wrongdoing, but rejoices with the truth. Love bears all things, believes all things, hopes all things, endures all things. Love never ends."

1 Corinthians 13:1–8

Epilogue

Even today, Joe and Brad continue to meet regularly. However, in addition to morning coffees, they now share emails and texts about what they are learning and how they are progressing.

If you would like to listen in or read about their conversations—or even participate with them—join them on https://joeandbrad.com. There's no charge to listen in.

Who knows, your life might be changed—maybe even more than Brad and Joe's.

END ?

About the Authors

Carl Bromer
Apollo Lunar Program Technician, Electrical Engineer, USAF, F4-Phantom Fighter Pilot, Award winning sales and manufacturing executive for Texas Instruments, Hamilton Avnet Electronics, Eskco, and Leadership Management Inc., Cedarville University Adjunct, married 46 years, four sons. Home: Dayton, Ohio.

Jordan Winar
Chief Growth Officer known for doubling sales annually in multiple industries; Hi-tech, medical device, home improvement, etc. Cedarville University Graduate, Endurance sport junkie, Married, three children. Home: Austin, Texas.

Acknowledgments

From Carl

Several key people helped Jordan and me to shape this book into a work we truly believe will bring value to every reader… and even more important than that, we pray and believe it will bring honor and glory to our Lord.

Two men have especially contributed to the coherency of this work: Harold (Hal) Daniel, and Steve Compton. It was especially encouraging working with these men and with Jordan, knowing all three are also brothers in Christ. Steve's wife, Renay, provided excellent proofing and also valuable guidance on the readability of the final manuscript.

A tremendous thank you as well to my wife and best friend, Pam for talking me off the ledge when I whined or complained about not making progress, or spending hours rewriting accidentally deleted pages. She is the most significant person in my life and God has used her to give me a glimpse of His love for me. I thank Him for every moment He has given me with her—forty-six years and counting.

From Jordan

To my brothers and sisters who shaped me. To my sister Julie: she taught me hard work. To my sister Jill: she taught me that relationships are the true currency of life. To my brother Jared, a true man's man: while I don't say it enough, it will always be written here if you forget—I love you. To my sister Jubilee, the doctor of the family: we are all proud of you!

To my mom and dad: they developed me. My mom raised me and my four siblings with thousands of meals, practices, laundry, and endless hours encouraging us to make our lives count. Thank you, Mom!

My dad was an entrepreneur before it was cool. Thanks for the lessons and for showing me it's OK to take risks and how to outwork everyone around me. You taught me persistence and to do my best, having fun, and making a difference. The two of you made my childhood wonderful and I will cherish it—and you both—forever!

To my Cedarville University brothers, whom I have had the privilege to do life with since the day we graduated. It's been a ride: Iain, Justin, Drew, Josh, Kevin, Chad, Andrew, and Michael. And those adopted after graduating: Bradley, Mark W., Mark S., and Matthew. You mean more to me than you know.

To Mandy, my wife. You changed my life! You make me better every day, and I thank God for how beautiful you have made our life together!

And finally, my kids: London, Win, and Duke. It is my earnest prayer that you will each read this book and then develop like Joe, the salesman in our book—and ultimately, lead like Brad, the company owner in our book.

Testimonials

From people who attended live workshops where the principles taught in Seller to Stellar were being presented.

What a great training session! Absolutely the very best I've ever been to in 38 years of selling and sales managing.   Monte Patterson, ADESA, Texas

THE best class I have attended in 30 years of retail.   James A. Sroka, Colony Marine, St. Clair Shores, MI

I have 30 years sales experience and I found the program energizing… It gave me a renewed attitude. Bob Johnson, ADESA-Cincinnati

This was by far the best sales training course I have attended. Thank you.   Todd Perry, Professional Micro Care, Dayton, OH

This is more than a "refresher" for me. It is the best one-day seminar I've ever attended. To merely say I learned a better way to sell is a huge understatement and a disservice. I was captivated by the strength of using just basic principles of behavior to achieve remarkable sales success. whether a person is out to improve product or service sales, negotiating mergers and acquisitions, conducting a job search, or any number of situations where buying and selling is practiced, the concepts you presented are powerful. Equally important, they can be easily carried out in day-to-day activities. This point is especially significant when we consider rival programs which present fine theory but cannot confirm their relevance in "real-world" situations. Unfortunately, over the years, I have attended several such programs. — Ronald O. Braswell, consultant, Dayton, OH (formerly with Reynolds & Reynolds where he had P&L responsibility for over $300M)

This is the best sales training that I have received! Brad Kirkpatrick, Westbrook Mfg. Inc., Dayton, OH

Thank you … I have received many positive comments, not only from owners of our company, but also from the sales force (inside and outside). It is highly unusual in our business to receive an order on the first call. However, right after taking your course one of our salesmen closed an order worth more than $100,000 on the first call. I suspect that salesman's selling techniques have been forever altered.   Stan Bell, Group Mgr., Batson Yarn and Fabrics Machinery Group, Greenville, SC

Excellent executable ideas to help me be more successful. Stefanie Savino, Cap Gemini, Dayton, OH

A confidence builder! I now know what to say when I'm told "No." Invaluable training! Jamie Wexler, Lexington, KY

This relates to all positions in our workplace. This is not just for your "typical" salesperson. It relates to a much larger spectrum of people. Scott Stalder, General Sales Manager, Los Angeles, CA

These principles and techniques speak to professionals in both large and small businesses who are involved in sales or sales management. I highly encourage you to consider it for your people.

Maureen Patterson, (Former VP, Member Relations) Dayton Ohio Area Chamber of Commerce

After attending Robbins, Ziglar, etc. this is the most well-thought-out correct sales program that I have had the opportunity to be involved in! Justyn Amstutz, ADESA

Great sales training. Great motivator to strive to improve in all areas of sales. Cynthia Jones, Nashville Convention Center

I appreciated your reference to upholding ethics and integrity. Too many salespeople are lacking in character. Renae Christofferson, Wyndham Hotels & Resorts, Nashville, TN

Best sales seminar I've attended. Professional, concise, and informative with practical tools for success. John Newton, People Network, Atlanta, GA

Being in Accounting, I have a newfound respect for Sales! Pat Hollingsworth, ADESA

Your program, without question, is the finest I have seen in 30 years of sales and sales management. I highly recommend this course for you – regardless of your industry, assuming you're looking for a course that will produce bottom-line results. Scot DeButy, President, Valcom Driver Leasing, Inc., Jacksonville, FL

Excellent presentation. Cohesive and comprehensive. Donna Snider, Baptist St. Vincent's Occupational Health, Jacksonville, FL

This had to be one of the best sales seminars I have ever attended. (And I have been to quite a few.) The straightforward, no-nonsense approach to your selling concept was second to none. I have <u>dramatically</u> increased my closing ratio. Move over Zig Ziglar, there's a new sheriff in town. Chris D. Estep, Client Service Mgr., Thompson Financial Services, Dayton, OH

The principles you teach relate to all industries and all levels of experience in sales Gloria Staton, Metro Atlanta Chamber of Commerce, Atlanta, GA

TESTIMONIALS

Thank you so much for your exceptional training program ... I have heard nothing but positive responses from it. ... Your natural concepts are great! Jack Novotny, Vice President, Crown Engineering, Dayton, OH

I really enjoyed your fast-paced and practical approach to the sales process. ... We can really apply your ideas to our day-to-day experiences. Nancy L. Graff, Director of Sales, BB Riverboats, Port of Cincinnati, Covington, KY

I came into this program with some reservation. Have been to many and thought it was the same old thing - - boy, was I wrong!! This was great!! Richard Quake, ADESA

As an employee of Motorola, Inc., I am required to complete a specific amount of training time each year. Many of those hours consist of courses taken within our own corporate training organization. We are encouraged to seek external learning opportunities that help us grow professionally. I have nineteen years' experience in selling ... The principles in your program came along at just the right time for me. I would recommend this to anyone with any level of sales experience. Dave Steinwert, Motorola, Cincinnati, OH

Very real world and easy to follow. Jay Buten, Fifth Third Bank, KY

Great class. It was never boring or dragging. Mike Moran, OKI Systems, KY

I've been in quite a number of sales seminars. This is the best I've ever experienced! Allison Arbogast, Hi-Gear Co., KY

A very practical approach to sales. This seminar empowered me to help build my business in areas I haven't tried before. It was excellent! The stories and visuals kept me alert all day. Lori Laake, Anything's Possible, Dayton, OH

This is my second time to take the program. It was valuable for me as a "rookie" salesman but even more valuable since I have acquired some experience. I have enjoyed it very much. Mark Allen, Dayton Nut & Bolt, Dayton, OH

This was the best sales seminar that I have attended ... and accomplished more in 8 hours than others that take 2 or 3 days.

Chuck Hays, Louis P. Batson, Inc., Greenville, SC

I have been struggling with an inexperienced sales team. This seminar was very timely for me and for them. Tracie Stafford, Greater Greenville Chamber of Commerce, SC

This has been the best sales seminar that I have attended as far as practical applications. Jim and Carl did a good job keeping the attention of everybody at the seminar. Jay Swetenburg, L. P. Batson Co., Greenville, SC

I have been to several sales seminars and *"Natural Selling Concepts"* gives the most realistic ideas and outline to improve my sales methods. Parker Moore, I H Services, Greenville, SC

Fantastic course, applicable but not "hoaky". Informative with great content, no wasted time on silly, interactive segments. Serious yet fun. Tonya Crist, Kahn Construction, Greenville, SC

Your seminar has helped improve my sales. I now better understand the "natural" flow of selling from generating rapport, handling objections, to gaining commitment, and doing follow-up. Your course has helped me increase my sales significantly. I just had my best two months back-to-back with a 40% increase from all previous months! I can't sleep on Sunday nights now! I say crazy things like "Thank God It's Monday!" I'm even more excited to get out and sell now that I have more knowledge of the sales process and actual techniques I can use. Certainly anybody doing outside sales could benefit from your course. I think inside salespeople and customer service representatives would benefit as well. Billy Anderson, Membership Development, Northern Kentucky Chamber of Commerce, Covington, KY

Until I started using the technique you taught on how to leave an effective voice mail, I rarely had a call returned from leaving one. Now I do, and it is so exciting! I've also experienced success in actually talking with the person on the phone and getting an appointment for a face-to-face meeting. Thank you so much for the training. It is one of the most important and impressive events I have been a part of, and now, it's part of me. Marcia Jensen, Satellink Communications

Thank you for the Sales Training Seminar you held in Atlanta. I keep the seminar workbook in the front seat of my car and read sections of it regularly when "parked" in Atlanta traffic. Recently I used your Pre-Qualifying Contract approach by offering a prospect an estimate (instead of the full-blown proposal.) By uncovering an upfront budget issue before we spent time on the full-blown proposal, I saved about nine hours of proposal writing time. That's approximately a $1,000 cost of internal resource time. Thanks! Don O'Sullivan, INSOL, Atlanta, GA

Other sales seminars I have attended have not been as straight forward and common-sense as yours. Thank you for helping me in my selling career. Frank Igleski, Akers Packaging Service, Chicago, IL

Many seminars I attend are bland and mundane. However, this seminar provided useful information in an energetic environment. I rate it a strong "10+" Thomas McBroom, Atlanta Gas Light Co.

I really could have used this course a few years ago! I can't thank you enough for sharing your insight and experience. Michael Crowley, The Fitness Store, Cincinnati, OH

I'm excited about returning to work with all of the concepts you covered. Your advice on how to handle "sticky" situations or how to avoid them was excellent. Mary Lynn Peacher, Pinetree Country Club, Kennesaw, GA

One of the first things you did was to request that each of us commit to reviewing our notes at least three times in the next two weeks. I take commitments seriously, so I did review my notes. As a matter of fact, upon reviewing my notes I realized that there was so much good information contained within them that I actually reviewed them five times in the immediately following two weeks. The information you present is interesting, uncomplicated, logically organized, and most of all relevant. It has helped me and my sales career will benefit. I highly recommend your training to anyone working in sales or other areas where they must interact and communicate with other people regularly. Derick Harper, Sales Mgr., Harper Oil Products, Inc., Florence, KY

I have applied your selling technique to my tele-sales calls and have found them to be very successful. The new approach and technique have been very gratifying and rewarding. I've seen immediate results and successful sales calls. I highly recommend this course to others in sales. Marie Gaudet, Lighting Systems, Warminster, PA

The *"Natural Selling Concepts"* class was a big hit with our sales force. We had people that have been selling for over 30 years attend your class, and they came out talking about how good this class was. A week after the class, I had one of the "old timers" come to me and say, "... I have been trying to sell this one account for about a year now and I used some of the concepts and THEY REALLY WORK!" ... I feel that your class is head and shoulders above all the classes I have attended. Dan Garrett, Marketing Mgr., Synthetic Industries, Inc., Chattanooga, TN

The program was fantastic! I've attended more of these than I can or want to remember; yours was a breath of fresh air in a stagnant industry. Your approach and techniques are excellent. Thanks! Joe Finger, ADESA

I have been so fired up all day to utilize the new ideas and lessons that I picked up from your program. Windham Pridgen, Atlanta Chamber of Commerce, Atlanta, GA

Very good course for any inside or outside salesperson. Larry Wheeler, Rumsey Electric, King of Prussia, PA

You are offering a great service! Since I attended, my sales have jumped from $200,000 to well over $1,000,000 and growing! Kirk Brittain, TPC Printing & Packaging, Chattanooga, TN

Very efficient and concise! Glenn McCoin, IntelliNet, Atlanta, GA

Techniques were presented in a way that was memorable. I am new to selling and I thought the program provided me with tools that enable me to go out with confidence. Brad Morrell, Foundation Mortgage Corp., Atlanta, GA

The principles and values were honest, insightful, and encouraging. Derek Mitchell, Pro Brand International, Atlanta, GA

Great course! I learned more in one day than in my entire sales career (5 years)! Mike Bryan, Marietta Board of Lights & Water, Marietta, GA

Marketing and selling are extremely difficult for me ... Your program helped me tremendously ... Thank you! Chris Heller, Pine Valley Apts. / Garden Design, Marietta, GA

Extreme value! I've attended many through the years. Great approach. Tom Jinks, Micro-Plus Systems, Marietta, GA

Great seminar! Helped with my advancement and concepts in selling. Bry Burnham, Micro-Plus Systems, Marietta, GA

Extremely efficient. Great information and excellent tools for everyday usage. Melissa Egan, YMCA, Marietta, GA

Very educational and motivational. The program gave me a renewed energy to obtain my sales goals. Mike Mosgovoy, Southern Mounding, Kennesaw, GA

I recommend this program to new and to veteran salespeople! Patrick Davalos, Aspen Productions, Inc., Atlanta, GA

This program "hit home runs" with the issues it addresses. Greg Dillard, Interspace Office Furniture, Marietta, GA

Very motivational. Makes you think of other ways to present and view the whole process. Jane Pelt, Integrity Underwriters, Marietta, GA

Simply outstanding! Brian Krupa, Sixty Lakes Marine, Harrison Township, MI

Great training for accountants who typically aren't sales oriented. Definitely helped! Cheryl Flynn, Crisp Hughes Evans

This was one of the best classes I have been to in 15 years of boat sales! Carl Lane, Colony Marine, St. Clair Shores, MI

The best sales training course I have ever attended. Rob Stubbs, Colony Marine, St. Clair Shores, MI

One of... No... THE best class I have attended in 30 years of retail sales! James Sroka, Colony Marine, St. Clair Shores, MI

Very informative, keeping the basics in mind and explaining solid principles that can and WILL make a difference in my sales process! Bill Tripp, Colony Marine, St. Clair Shores, MI

Excellent course for Accountants who are not "natural" salespeople. This was not a subject offered in school! Melanie Watkins, Crisp Hughes Evans

TESTIMONIALS

This program was very good. I recommend it for those who experience difficulty knowing where to start when it comes to selling.   Fran Noel, Crisp Hughes Evans

I enjoyed the program. It not only gave me ideas to use at work but also in my personal life.   Joe Molis, Crisp Hughes Evans

Awesome! This is something any employee at any business can use.   Pat Scott, ADE-SA-Sacramento

Excellent course. First sales course that I experienced which taught me to improve myself to fit my system, not someone else's sales system. Thank You!!!   Tim Davis, Jackson National Life Insurance Co., Atlanta, GA

I've been through other programs on selling. Yours is the best!   Kevin Glass, Coalition America, Inc., Atlanta, GA

I have been in sales for 10+ years and been through many sales training programs. This was clearly the best one based on the delivery, content, and "no-nonsense" approaches and ideas.   Steve Noury, Coalition America, Atlanta, GA

I think that this course was more practical and addressed issues of the real world much more effectively than any others that I've attended.   Ed King, Louis P. Batson, Inc., Greenville, SC

Best sales course yet!   Dick Deahl, Louis P. Batson, Inc., Greenville, SC

Best sales seminar I have ever attended and I have been to several.   Ben Rushing, Louis P. Batson, Inc., Greenville, SC

I have never considered myself a salesperson, but your seminar changed that. You made it easy . . Not scary!   Trish Schenk, The Fitness Store, Columbus, Ohio

Excellent seminar - - should be absolutely mandatory for all sales staff.   Pat Goode, ADE-SA-Ark-La-Tex

www.ingramcontent.com/pod-product-compliance
Lightning Source LLC
Chambersburg PA
CBHW070602100426
42744CB00006B/378